SIXTY-SIX SHADES OF LIFE

J S Chahal

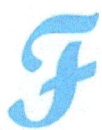

Copyright © 2022 J S Chahal

All rights reserved

The characters, narrative, description, and events portrayed in this book are fictitious. Any similarity to real persons, living or dead, is coincidental and not intended by the author.

The sole intent of the author is to amuse, foster creativity, delight, excite, inspire, motivate and promote reading.

No part of this book may be reproduced, or stored in a retrieval system, or transmitted in any form or by any means, electronic, mechanical, photocopying, recording, or otherwise, without express written permission of the publisher.

Cover design by: J S Chahal

Dedicated to Family and Friends

CONTENTS

Title Page
Copyright
Dedication
Prologue

Hue Highlighted Heritage House.	1
Rock-Solid Support	2
Blue Waters	3
Monkey and Milestone	4
Steadfast Stones	5
Road Mirage	6
Bird Walk	7
Heritage Building Brightly Illuminated	8
Steadfast Lamps Shining in the Storm	9
Exercise is Fun	10
The Pentagon Plant	11
Flower Firmament	12
On Top of the other Tasks	13
Healthy Foundation	14
Cherish Chaos	15
In Laughing Mood	16
Eleventh Hour	17

Monkey to Milestone	18
The Green Bell	19
Windows on History	20
Green in Green	21
Woods and Water	22
Eyeing the Sky	23
Pure Purple	24
Casting an Eager Eye	25
Lamp n Shade	26
Dreadnought Dinosaurs	27
Black n White	28
Flying High	29
Monkey Marathon to Milestone	30
Perfect Pot-work	31
Splitted but not Shattered	32
Stunning Shades	33
United We Stand	34
Swan Swim	35
Catnapping Crocodiles	36
Swan Swarm	37
Something Fishy	38
Spectacular Sunset	39
Out of the Blue	40
Peacock on Prowl	41
Shell Shocked	42
Snail	43
Caricature	44
Color Candor	45

Canine Conference	46
Watermark	47
Turning Back	48
Mountain Town	49
Beach n Palm	50
Black n White	51
Cloud Drift	52
The Sunset and Sea	53
Home Coming	54
Rainbow	55
Flower Power	56
Ruins in Red	57
Dance and Delight	58
The Sun Diving into Darkness	59
The Guard	60
Shrubs and Sunset	61
Golden Age	62
Flying Colors	63
Mustard Flower	64
Puppet at Play	65
Time-Piece of Advice	66
Scenic Seashore	67
Be your Best creative self	69
About The Author	71
Books By This Author	73
Looking Forward to your visit at	77

PROLOGUE

Sixty-Six shades of Life - is a rare collection of remarkable narratives blended with strikingly lifelike pictures.

Creative, powerful, and inspiring words have a profound impact on the mind. When combined with pictures, its effect on the brain is magnified and multiplied.

This collection of rare and inspiring pictures will foster creativity, amuse, excite, enthuse, encourage, inspire and uplift your mood, and boost your morale to achieve your personal and professional goals and objectives. Powerful words and images will leave an imperishable impression on your mind. Its long-lasting motivational effect will enable you, to live life to its full potential. The positive impact of these quotes will unleash your creativity renew, replenish, revitalize you and reduce stress.

You will be bewitched by creative words and beautiful pictures. And it is full of fun.

SIXTY-SIX SHADES OF LIFE
J S Chahal

HUE HIGHLIGHTED HERITAGE HOUSE.

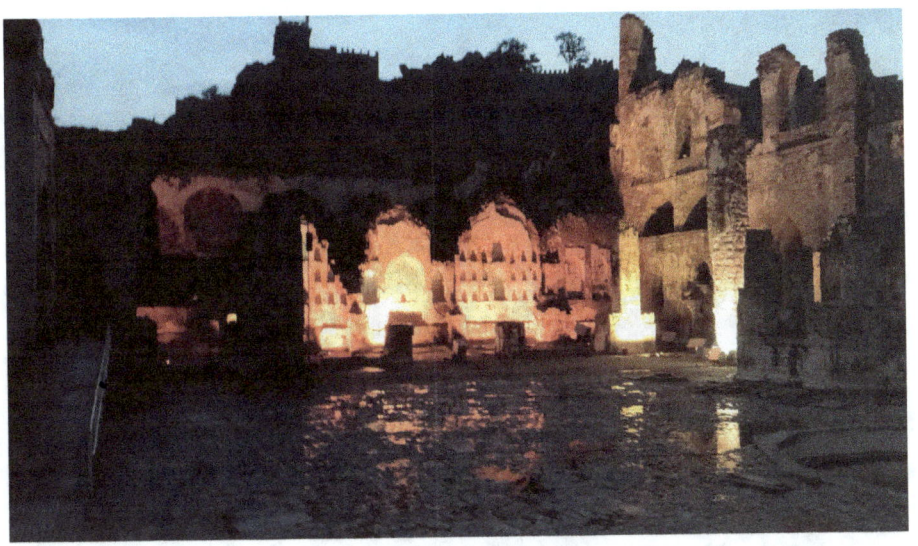

A Perfect Picture Portraying Preservation and Perseverance of old Heritage House - Highlighted by Hue.

ROCK-SOLID SUPPORT

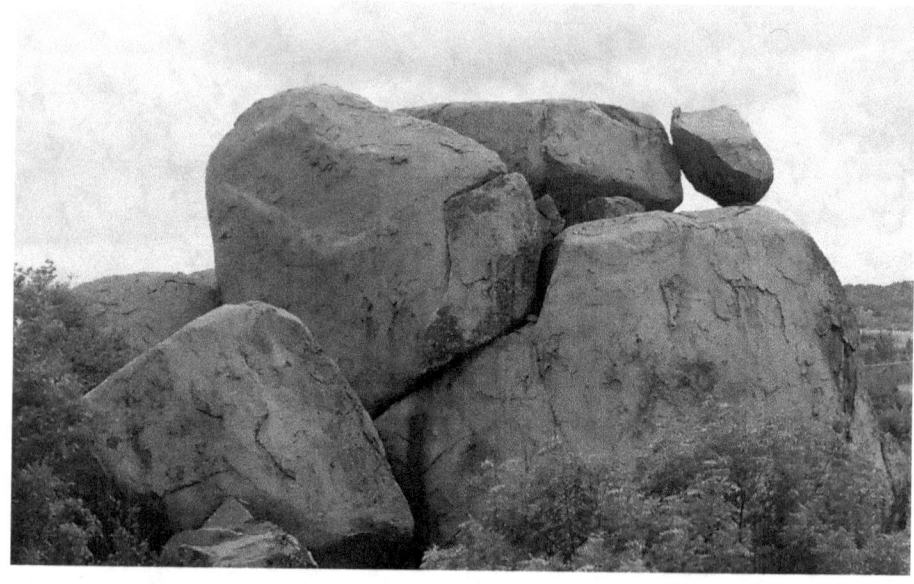

Stones providing Rock-Solid Support to each other. They may be broken but Spirit is not shattered. Teaching Humankind a valuable lesson - Support the other - when someone is about to fall. Stand steadfast!

BLUE WATERS

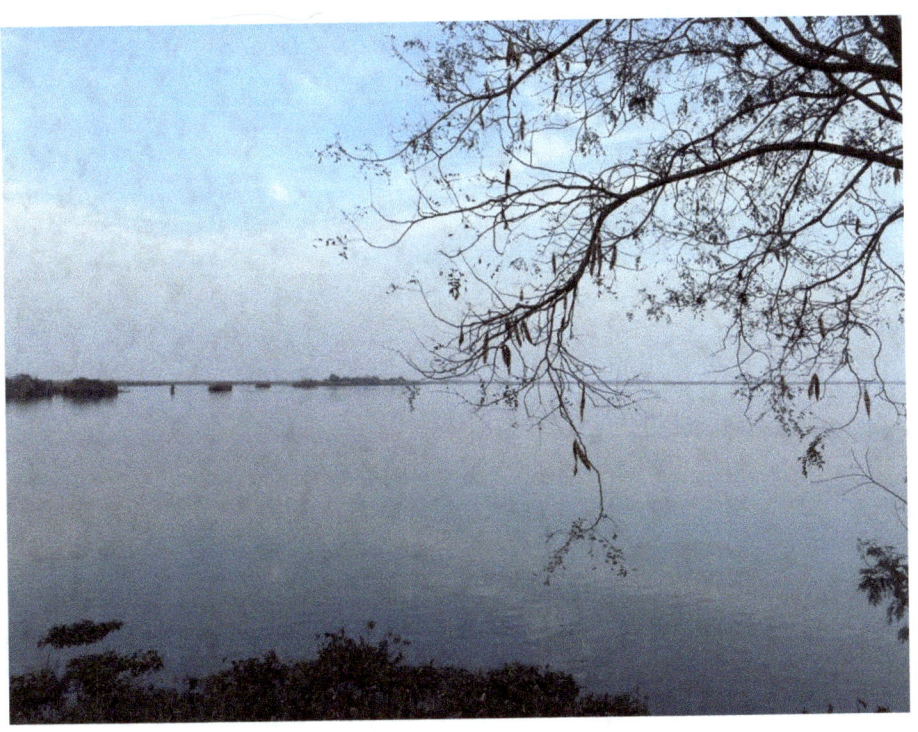

A Scenic Sky saturating Lake with its Sky-Blue Color. Silence Please!

MONKEY AND MILESTONE

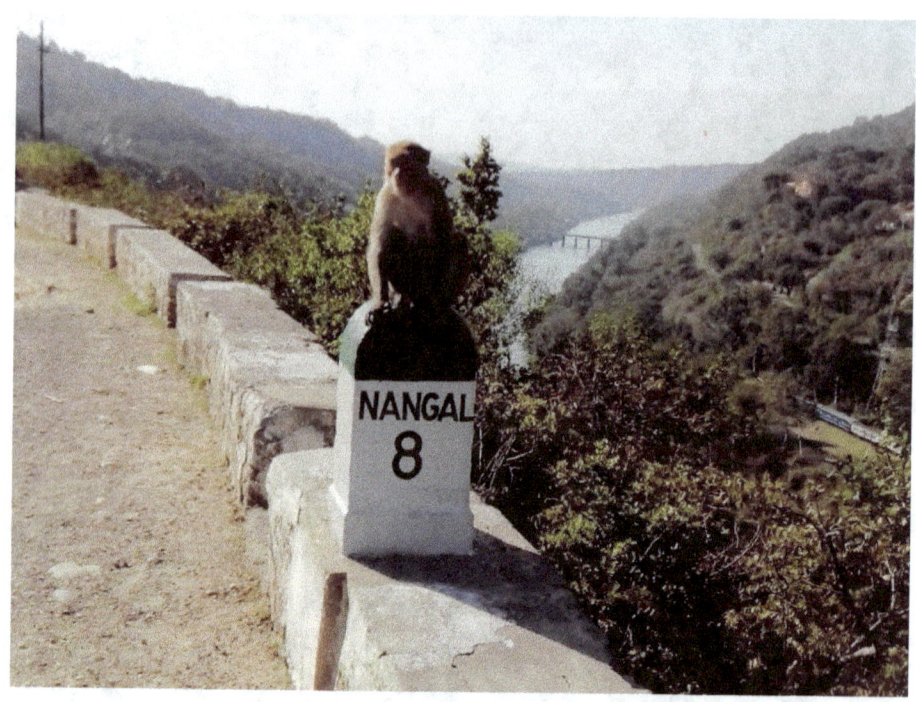

The Scenery is lovely, and River is deep. But I've promises to keep. Eight Miles to Go. Before I sleep.

STEADFAST STONES

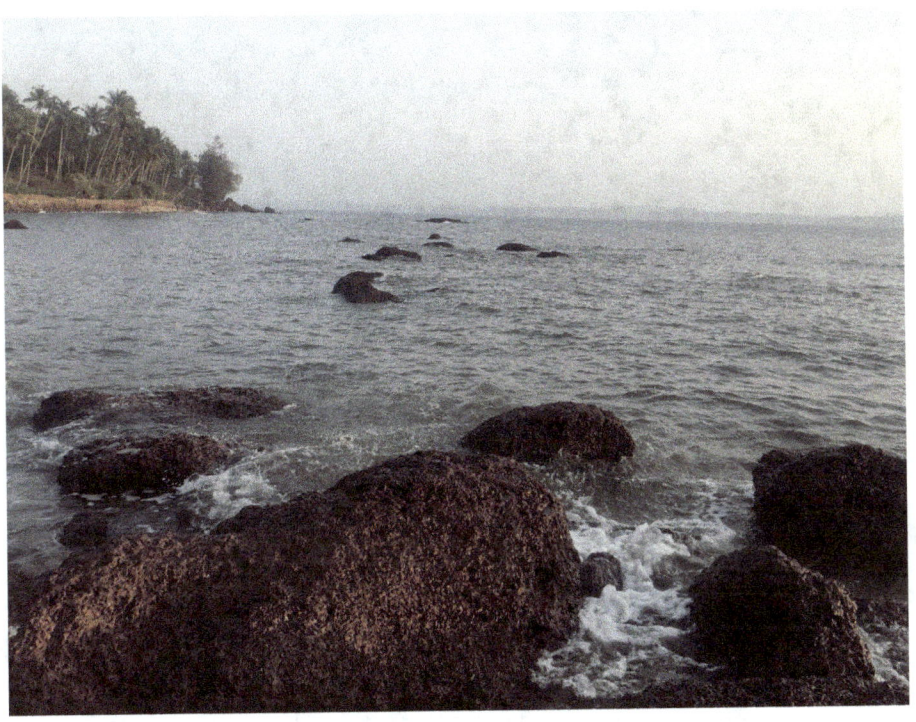

Steadfast Stones withstanding the onslaught of Salty Sea Water. Glowing by Sunset. Waving to Water Waves. Spreading Steadfastness and Radiating Resiliency. Spectacular Seascape.

ROAD MIRAGE

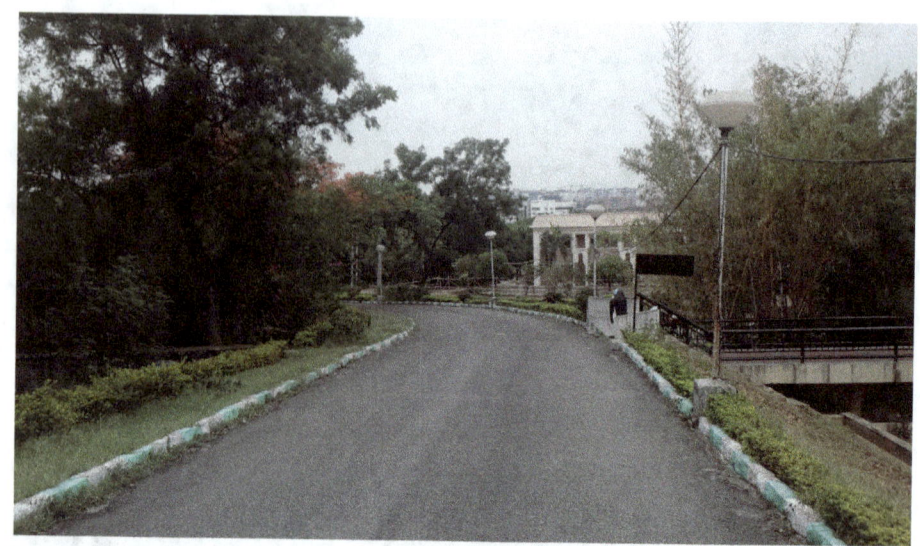

Mirage - Road appears to End - But it's the beginning. The road is entering the Startling Scenic Site. Likewise, many times in Life we think of a situation or Event as Deadened, whereas it might be the start of a new Wonderful Era.

BIRD WALK

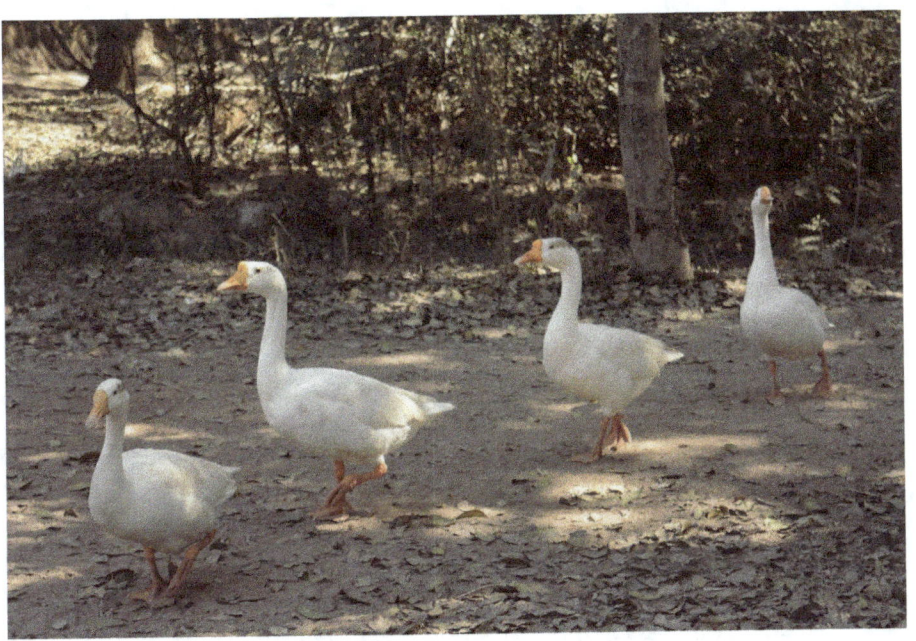

Bird Walk through Woods - A rare picture of Birds Walking in the Woods in Perfect Formation. Showing Leadership Skills!

HERITAGE BUILDING BRIGHTLY ILLUMINATED

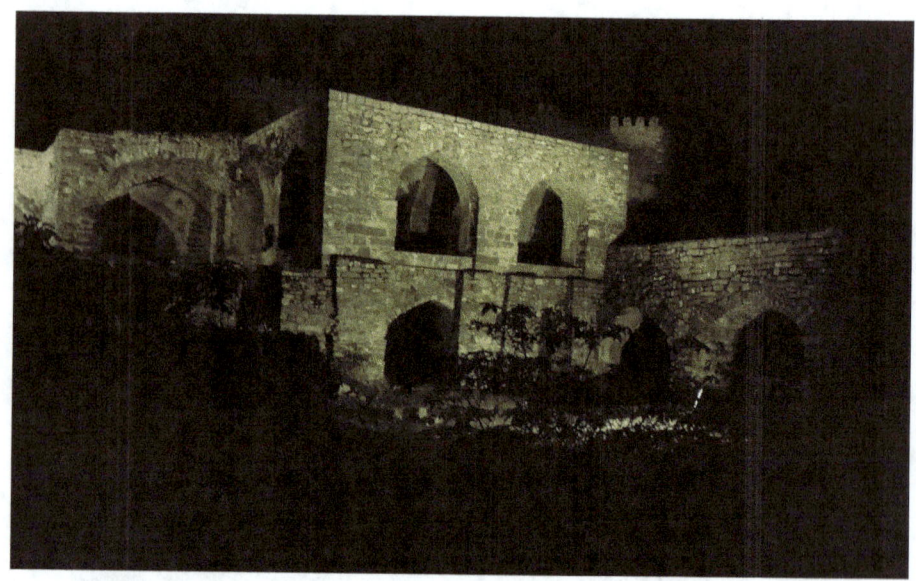

Heritage Building Brightly illuminated by Light - Defining Dark and Light Scenario. Throwing Light on History!

STEADFAST LAMPS SHINING IN THE STORM

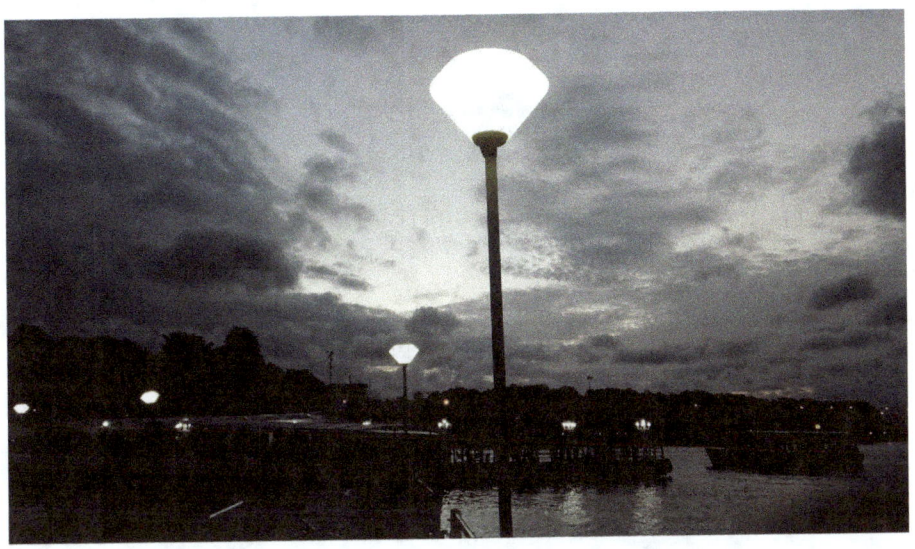

Steadfast Lamps Shining in Storm. Brightening the Dark Sky. Inspiring us and Radiating Resiliency.

EXERCISE IS FUN

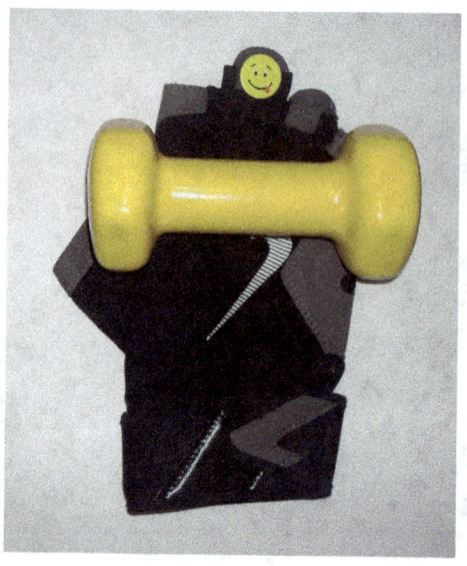

Exercise Promotes Health & Happiness. Just do it!

THE PENTAGON PLANT

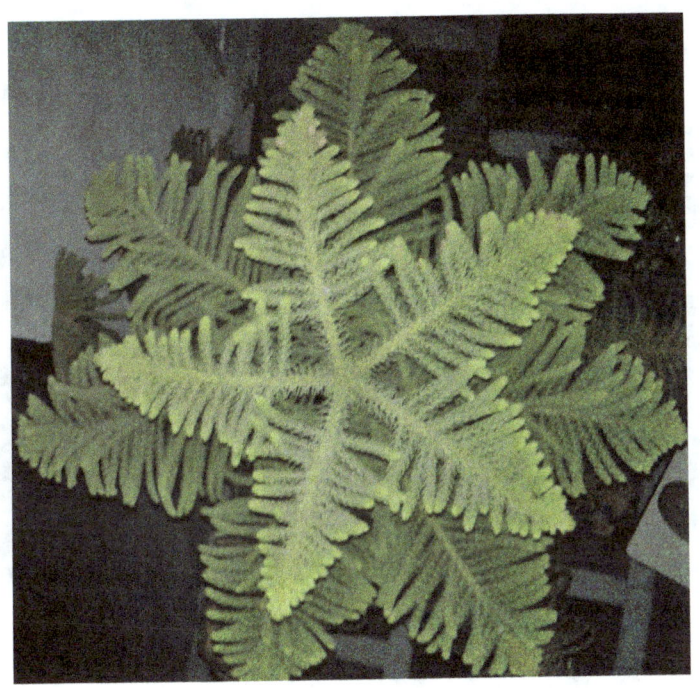

The Gleaming Green Pentagon Plant

FLOWER FIRMAMENT

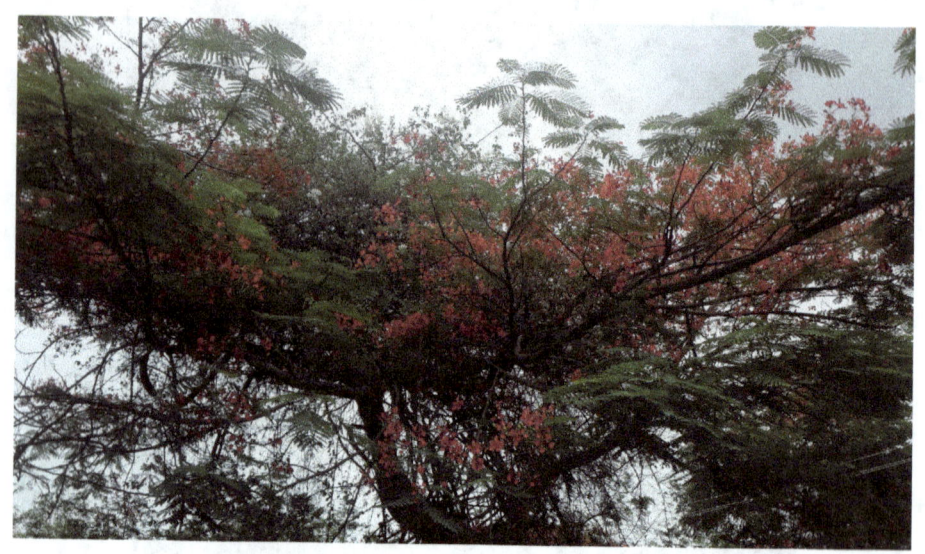

Flowers Firmament - These beautiful Red Flowers and Green Leaves - blur the Skyline.

ON TOP OF THE OTHER TASKS

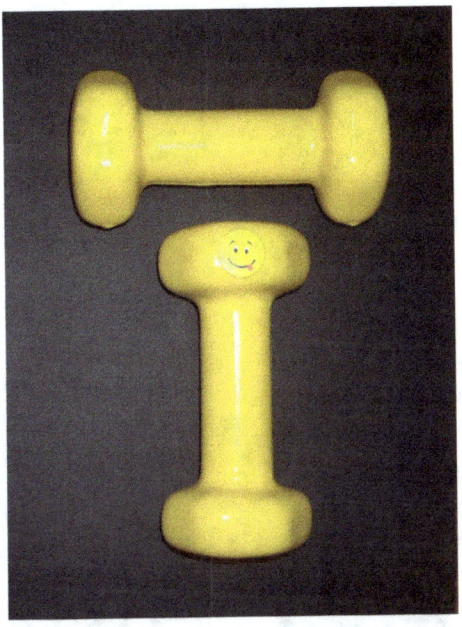

Even a little bit of Exercise promotes Health, Happiness, and Well-being. Put it on Top of the other Tasks.

HEALTHY FOUNDATION

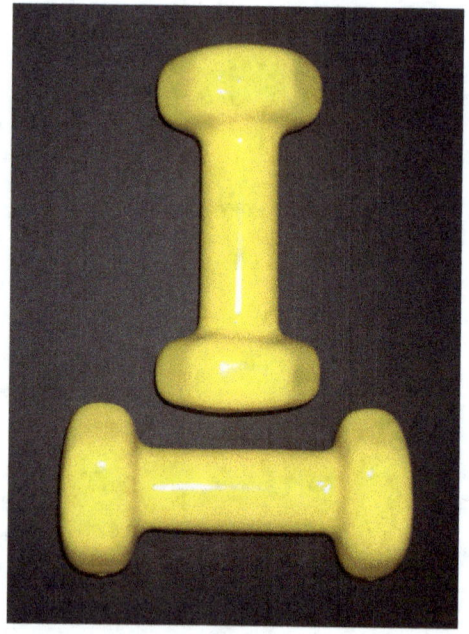

*Exercise provides a Healthy Foundation.
Just do it - Everyday.*

CHERISH CHAOS

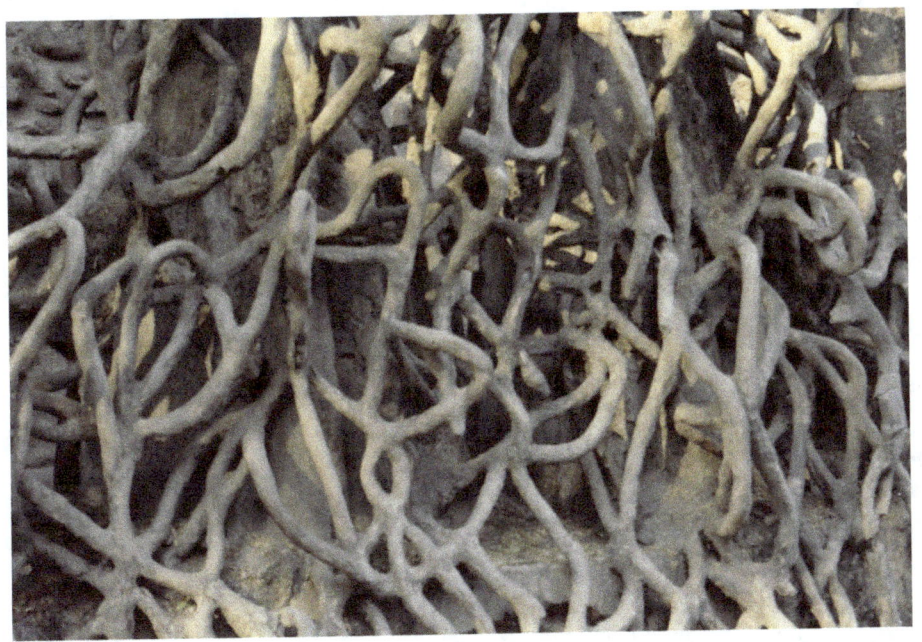

Life's Mess and Chaos. Enjoy and Cherish it!

IN LAUGHING MOOD

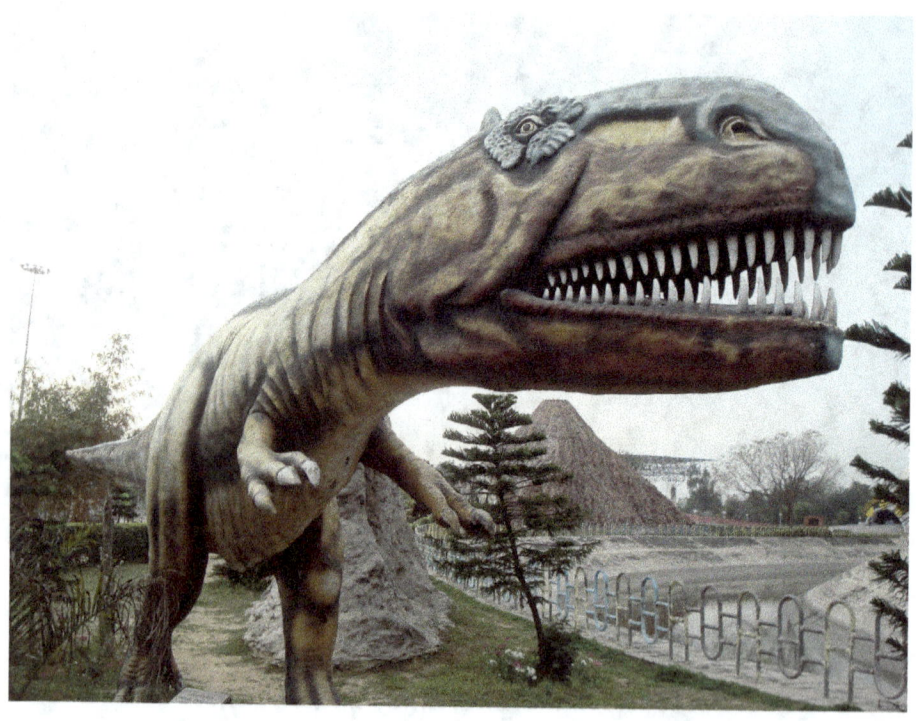

This Dinosaur is in Laughing Mood. Be Serious.

ELEVENTH HOUR

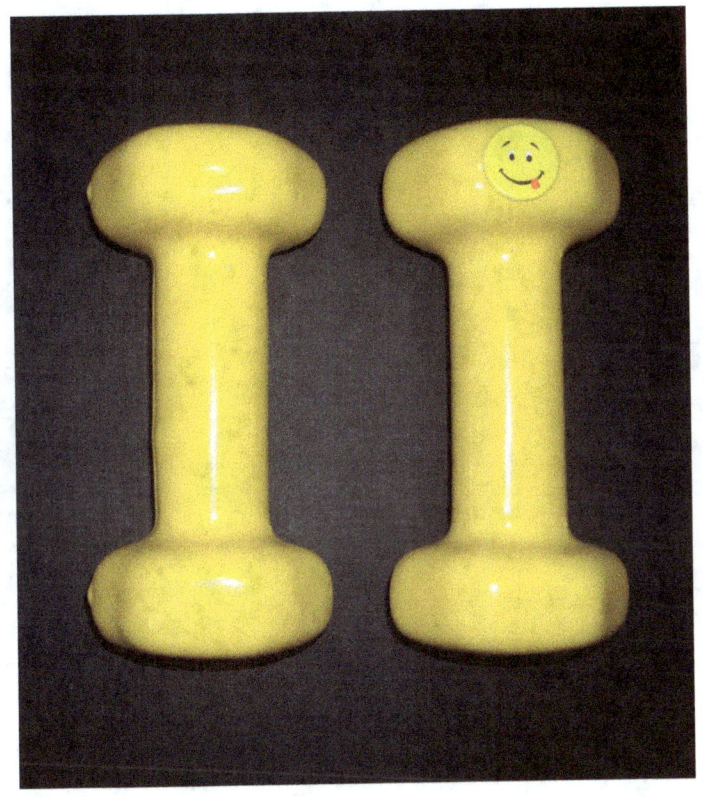

No time for Exercise? Do it even at Eleventh Hour. Before it is too late.

MONKEY TO MILESTONE

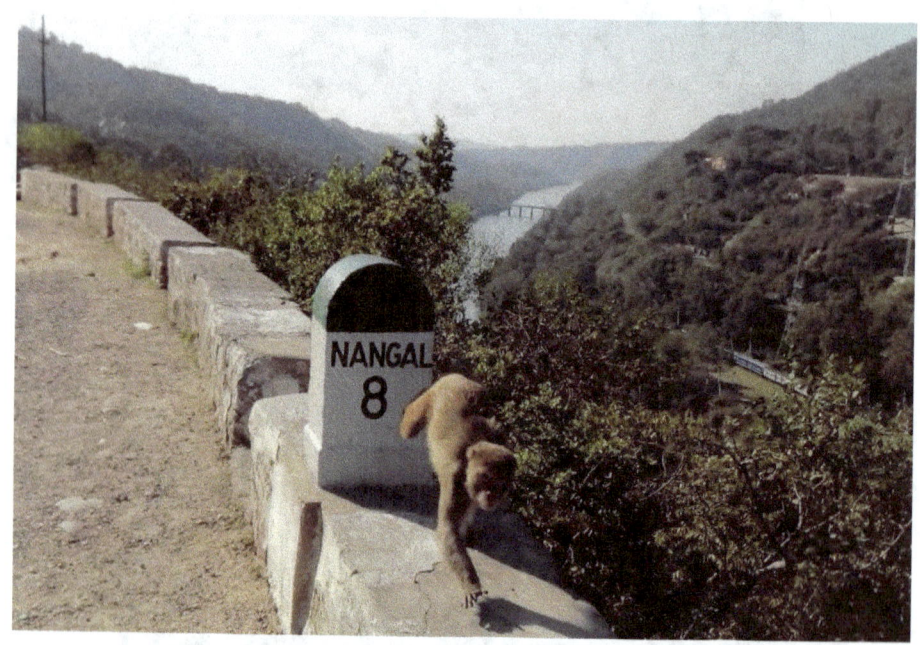

The Scenery is lovely, and River is deep. But I've promises to keep. Still, Eight Miles to Go. Before I sleep.

THE GREEN BELL

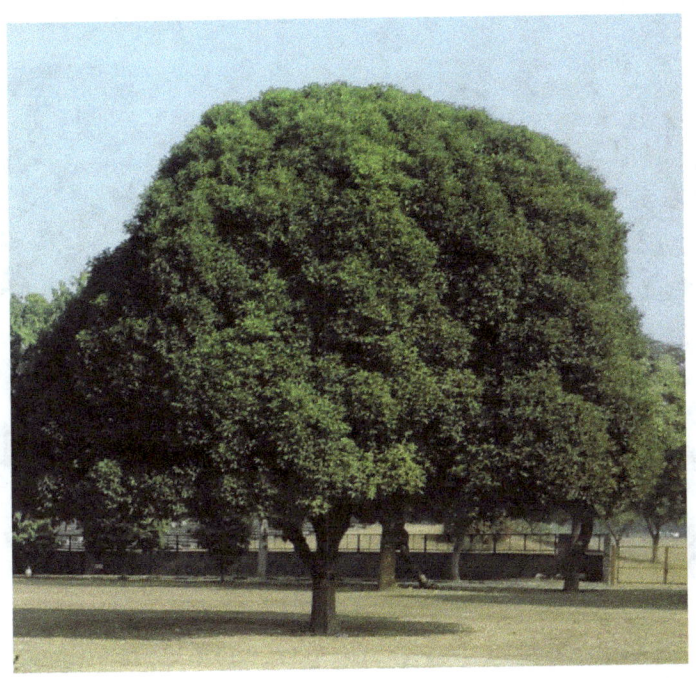

A lush green tree – bell-shaped. Raising Alarm for Conservation of Woods and Forest.

WINDOWS ON HISTORY

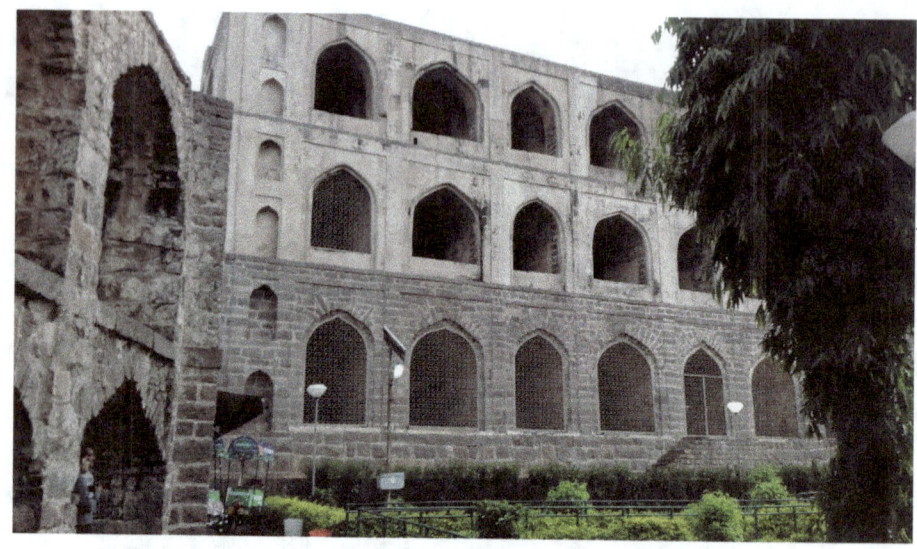

An Ancient Architecture Monument. A Heritage Building comprised of Arches. Windows on History.

GREEN IN GREEN

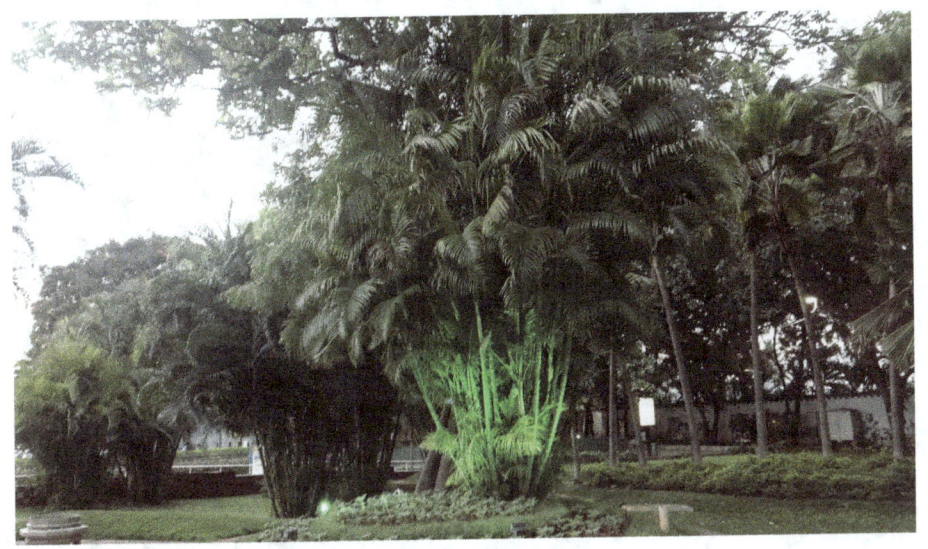

The Glowing Green in Green Shades. All Shades are Green.

WOODS AND WATER

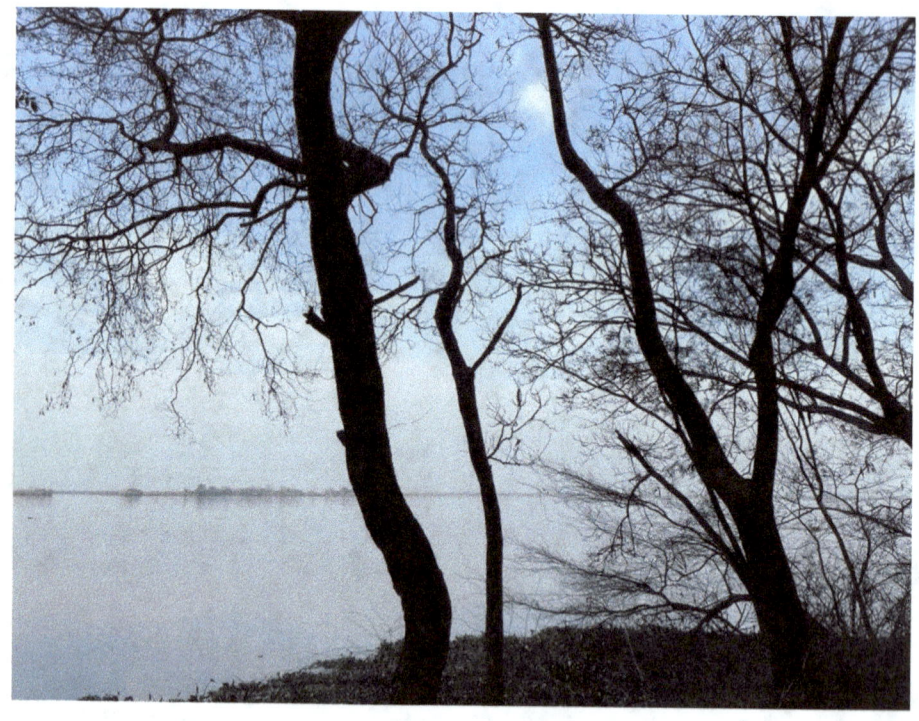

Woods and Water - beautiful woods in the backdrop of blue water.

EYEING THE SKY

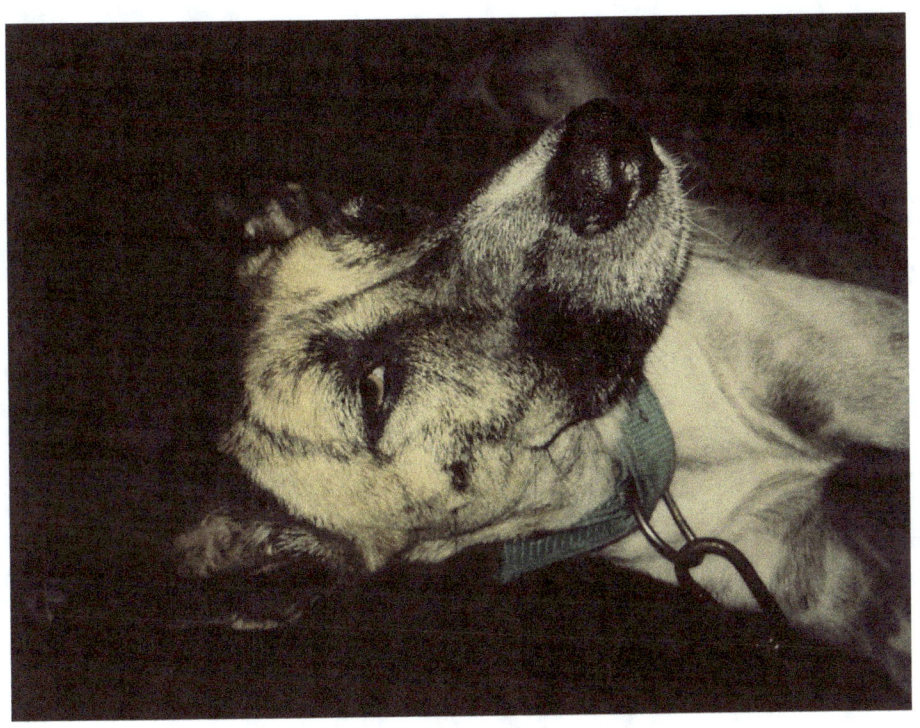

This pet with Stars in her Eyes is Eyeing the Sky.

PURE PURPLE

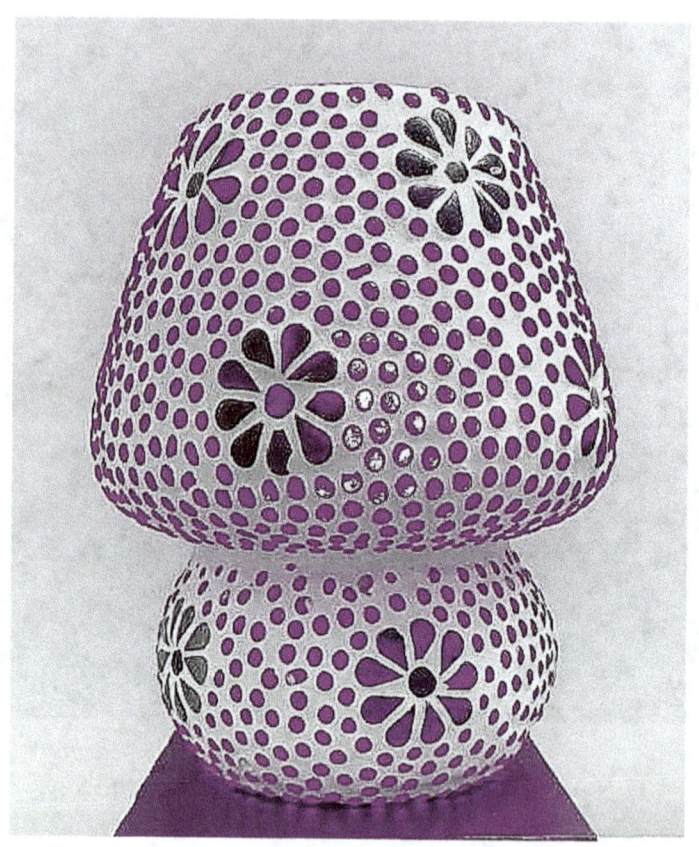

Sparkling lamp radiating brilliance

CASTING AN EAGER EYE

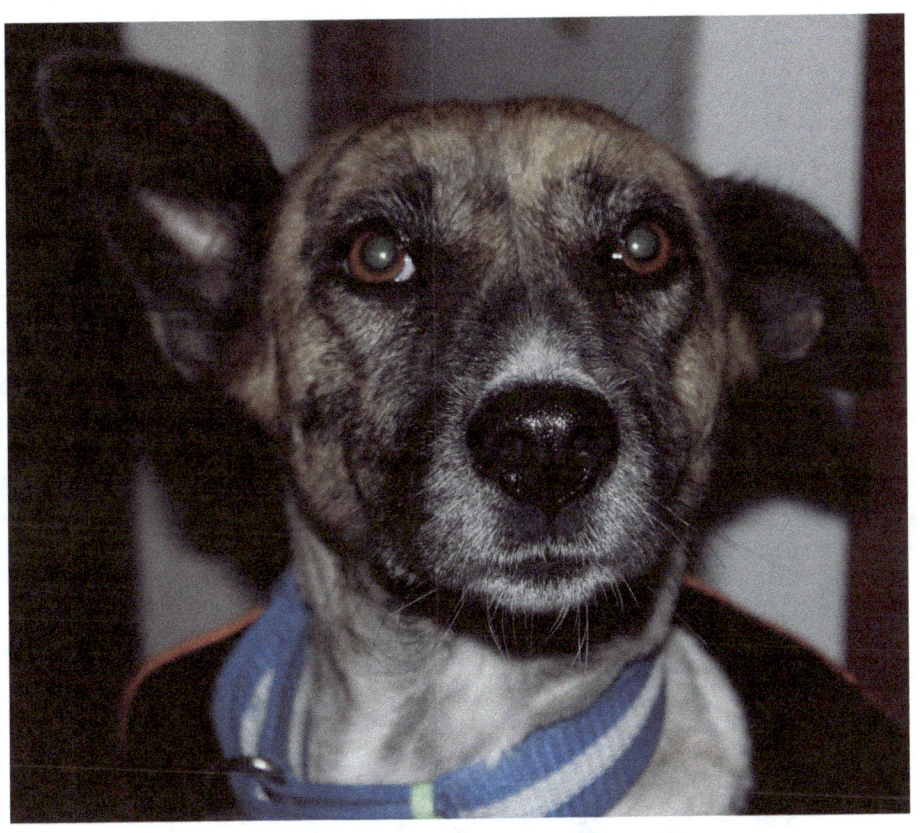

With an Eye to the Future - this pet is Casting an Eager Eye.

LAMP N SHADE

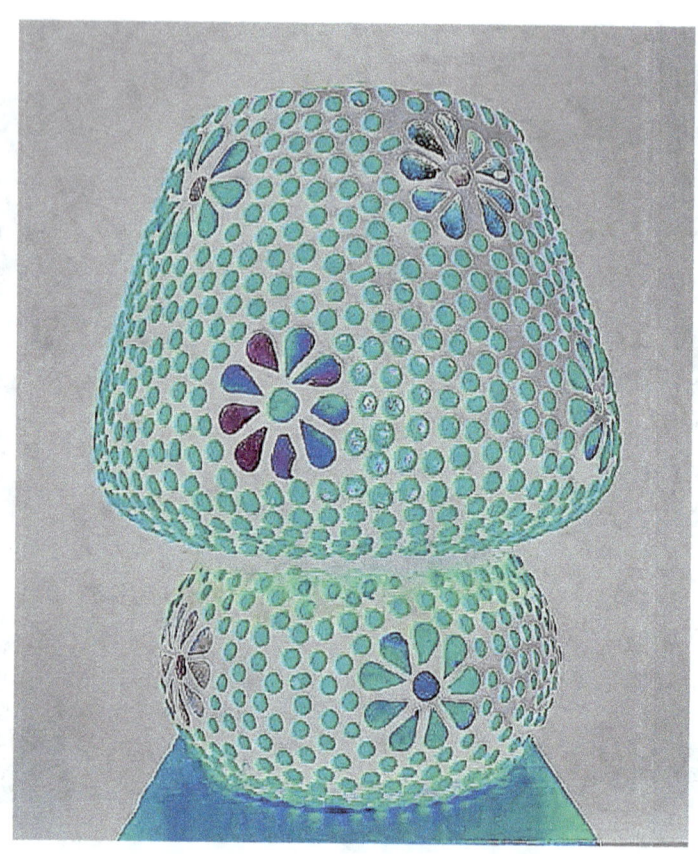

Sparkling lamp radiating brilliance

DREADNOUGHT DINOSAURS

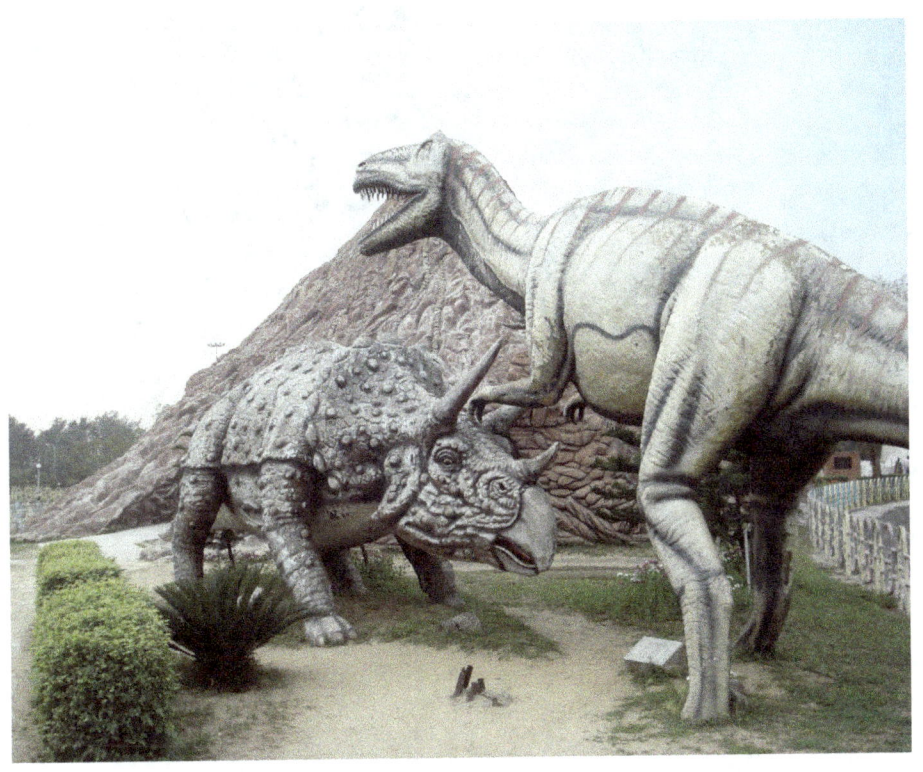

Dinosaurs searching for something to Dine.

BLACK N WHITE

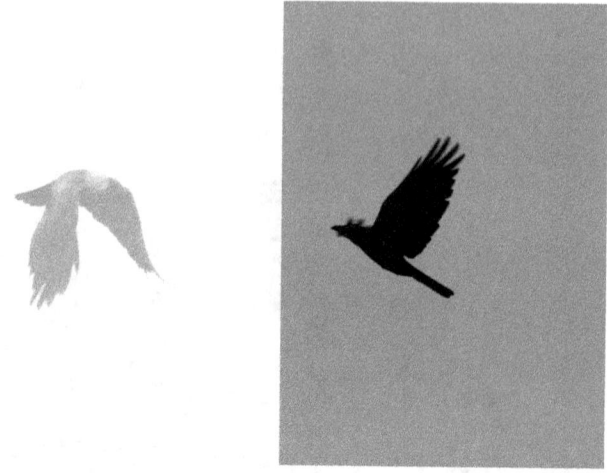

Flying Crow Captured in Black and White.

FLYING HIGH

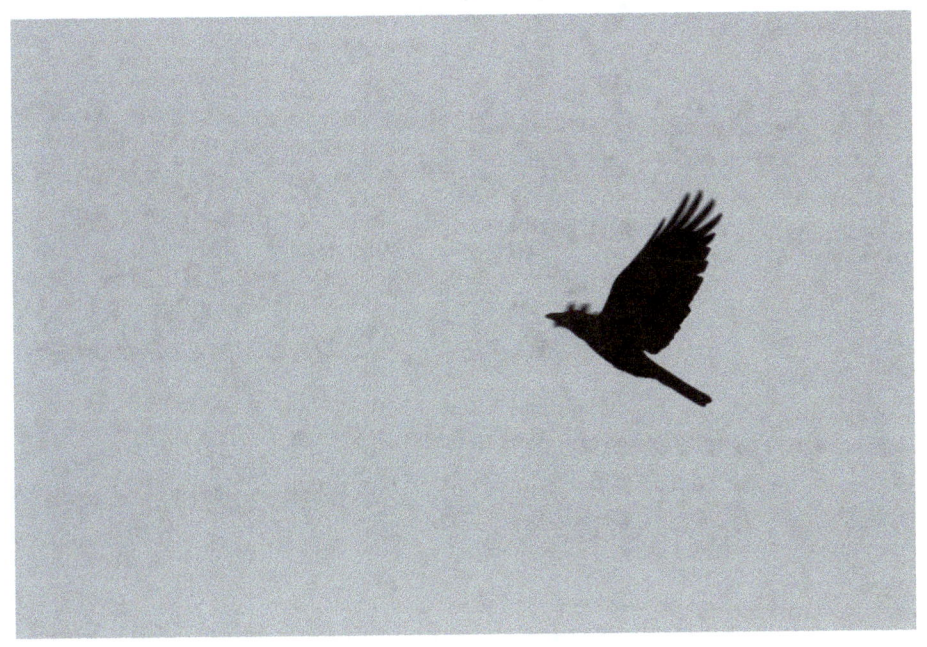

Taking off. The sky is no limit for this crow.

MONKEY MARATHON TO MILESTONE

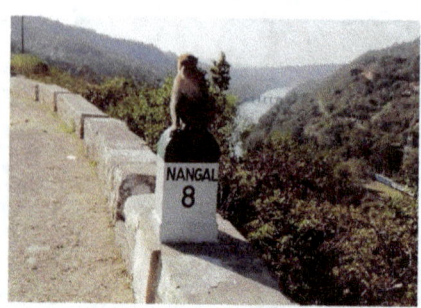 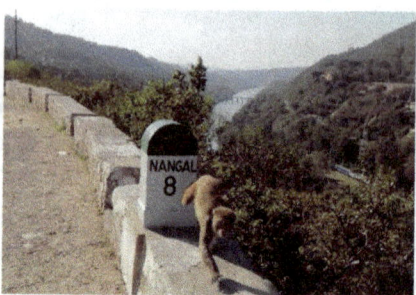

The Scenery is lovely, and River is deep. But I've promises to keep. Still, Eight Miles to Go. Before I sleep.

PERFECT POT-WORK

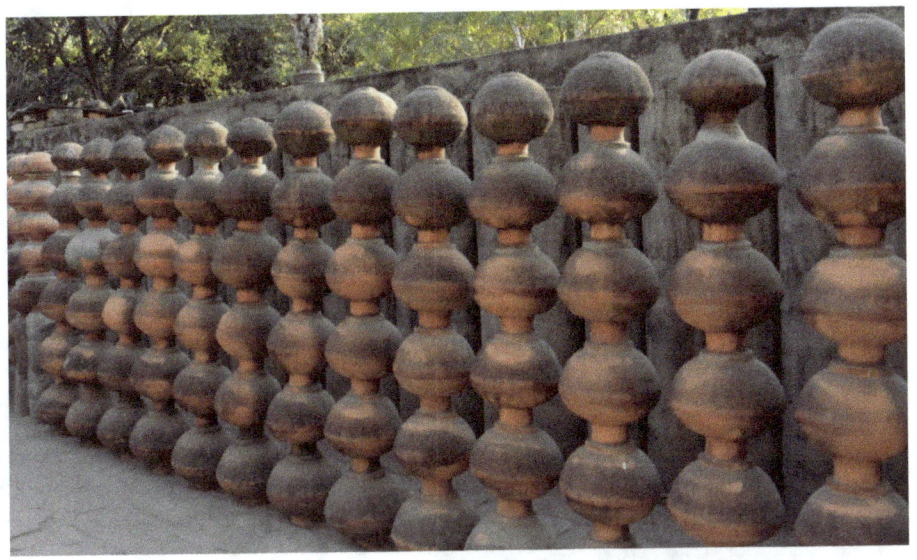

An Amazing Picture Portraying Perfect Pot-work.

SPLITTED BUT NOT SHATTERED

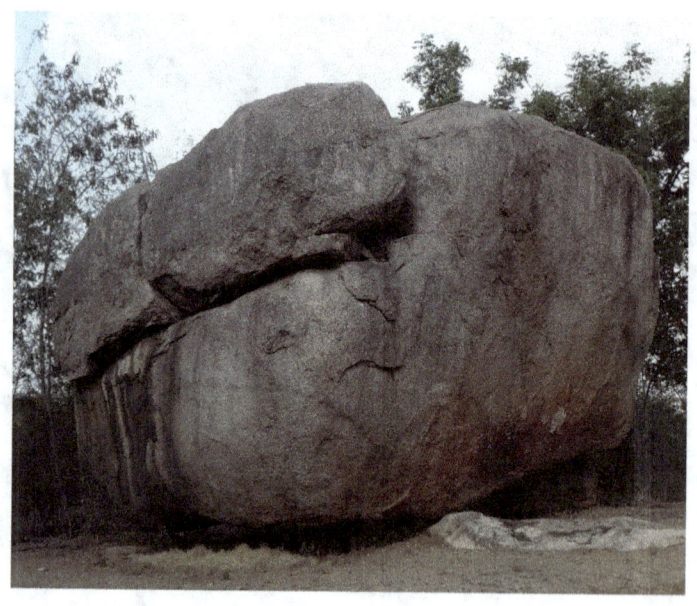

Splitted but not Shattered. Showing Strong Stony Spirit.

STUNNING SHADES

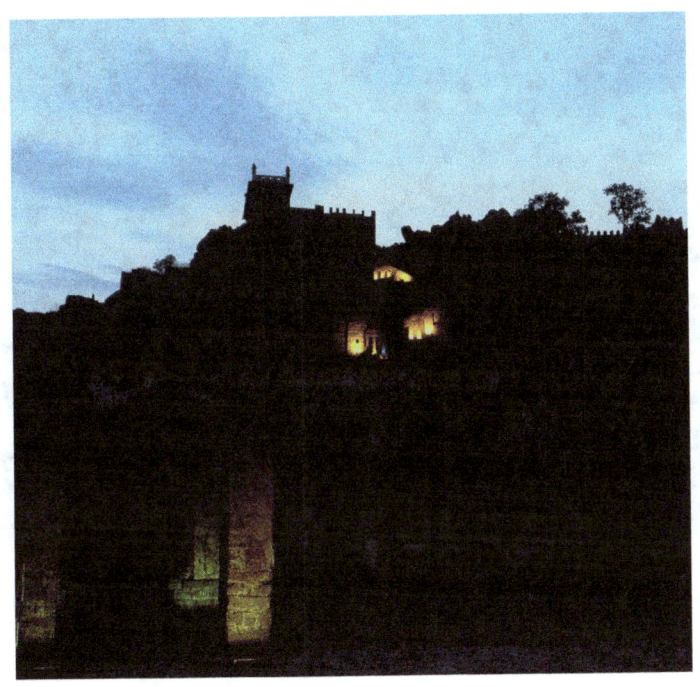

Stunning Shades and the Sky.

UNITED WE STAND

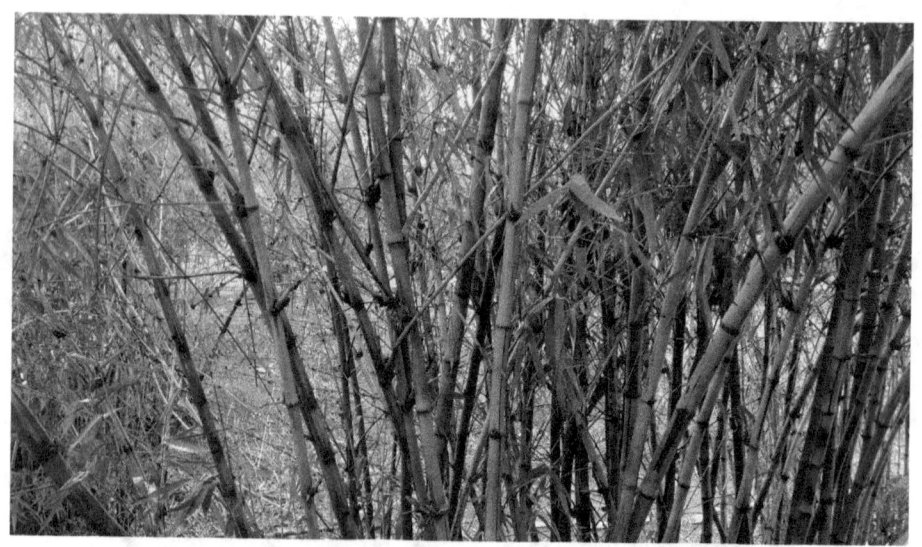

Beautiful Bamboo Shrub. Conveying United We Stand.

SWAN SWIM

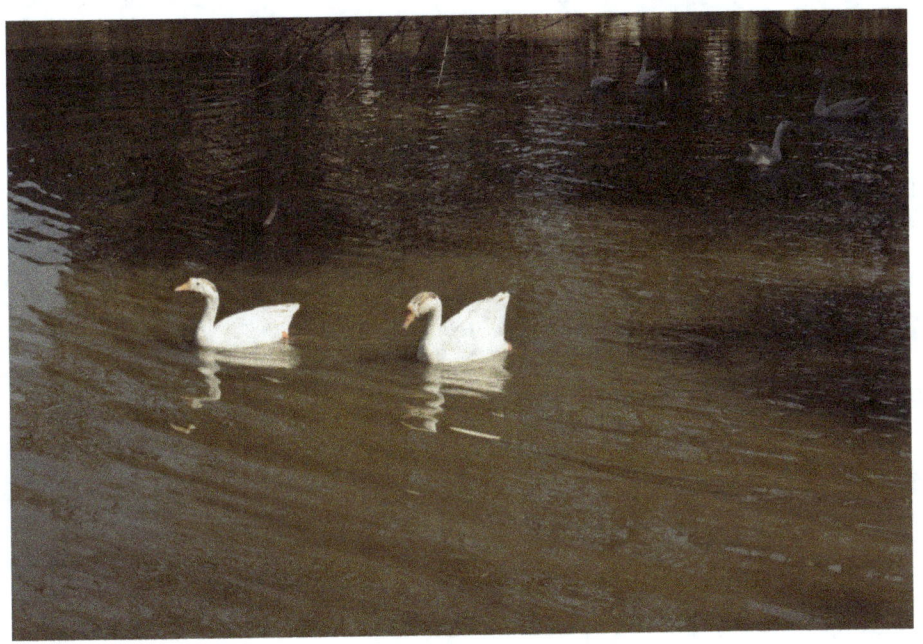

Bathing in Muddy Water. Still So White.

CATNAPPING CROCODILES

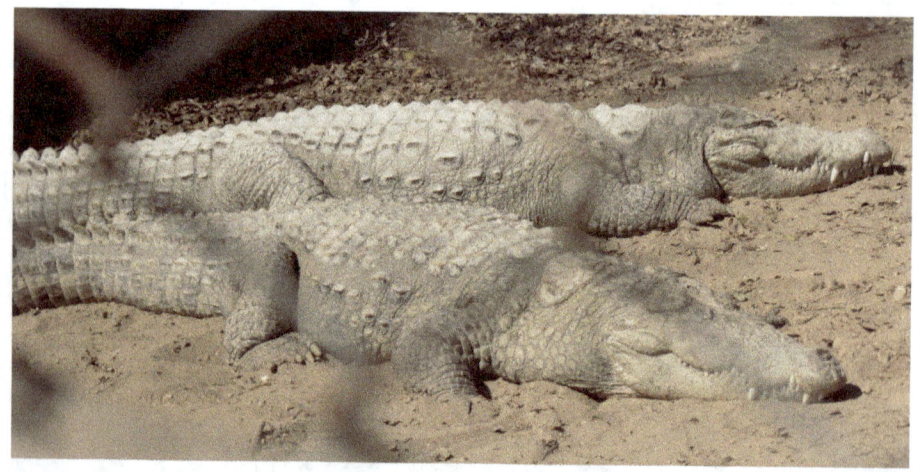

Calm and Catnapping Crocodiles.

SWAN SWARM

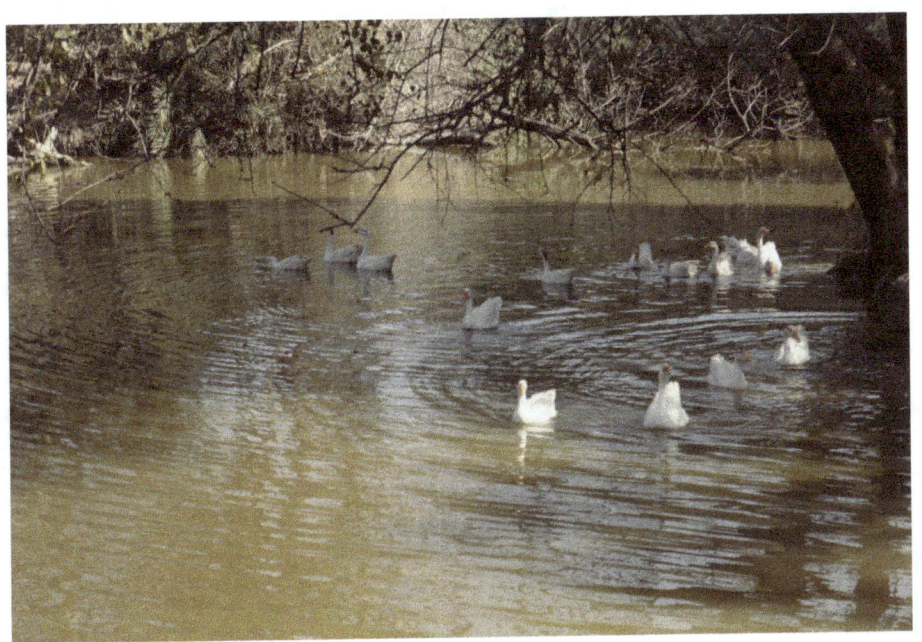

Swan Swarm

SOMETHING FISHY

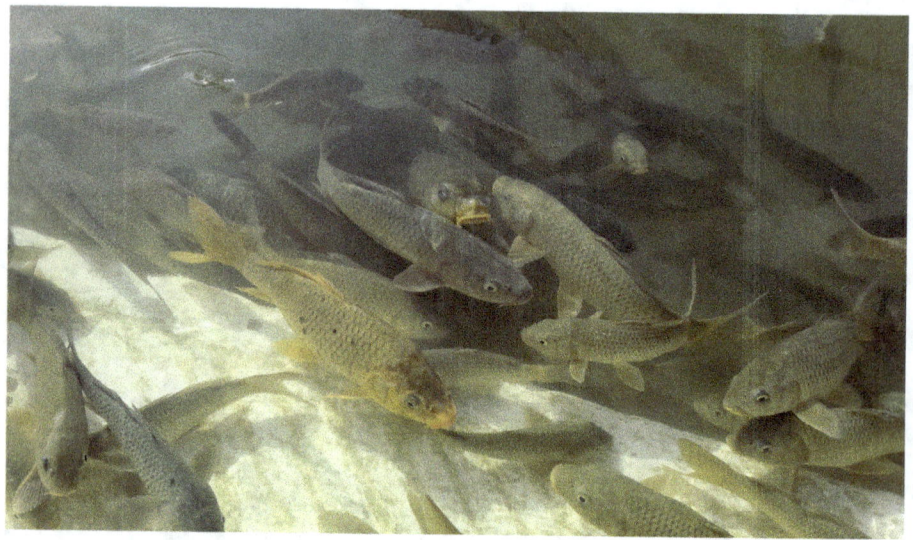

Fishes are finding something Fishy

SPECTACULAR SUNSET

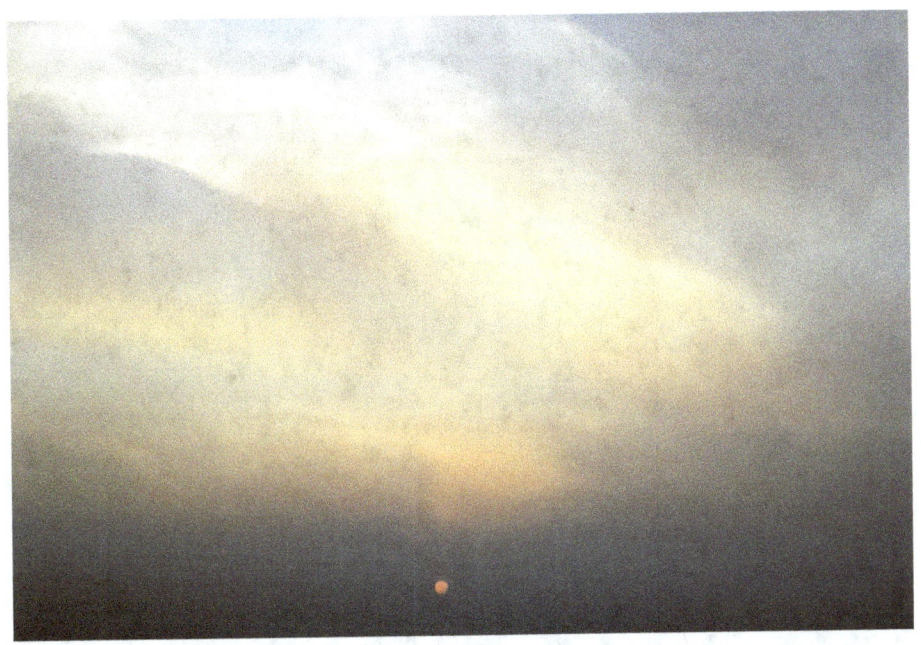

Scenic and Spectacular Sunset.

OUT OF THE BLUE

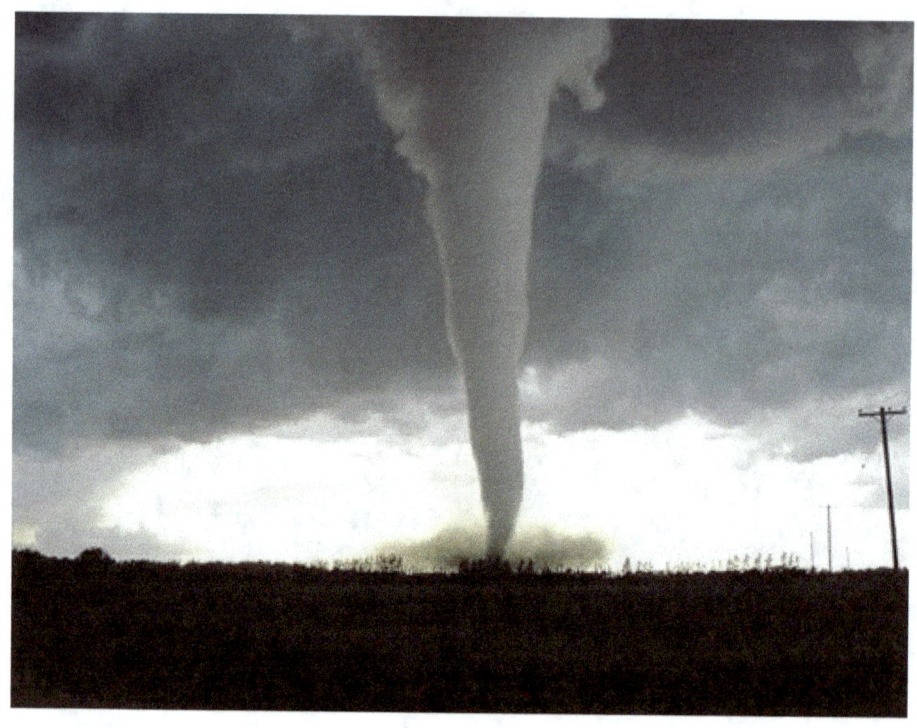

This tornado tempested without telling anyone.

PEACOCK ON PROWL

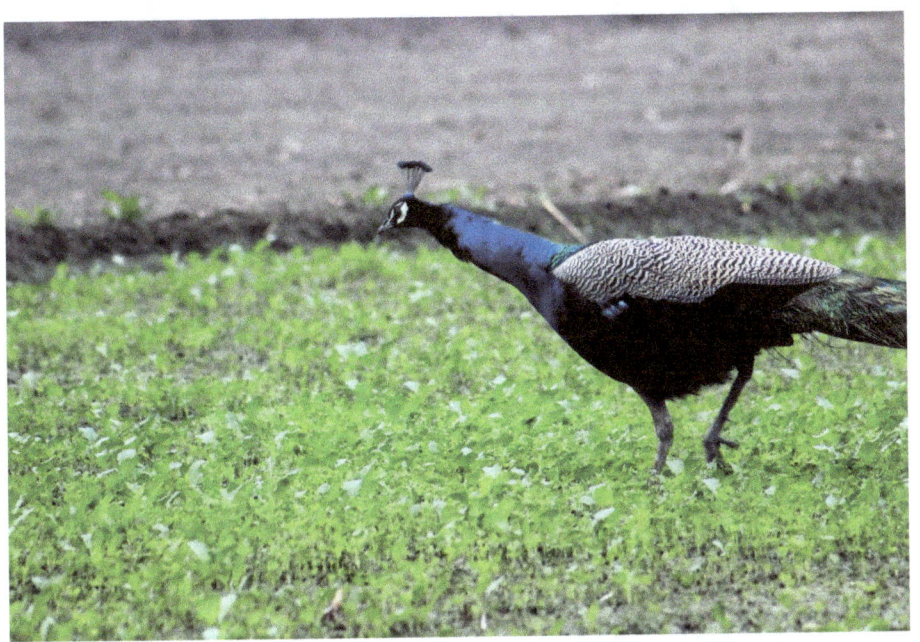

Peacock on Prowl - in search of Prey.

SHELL SHOCKED

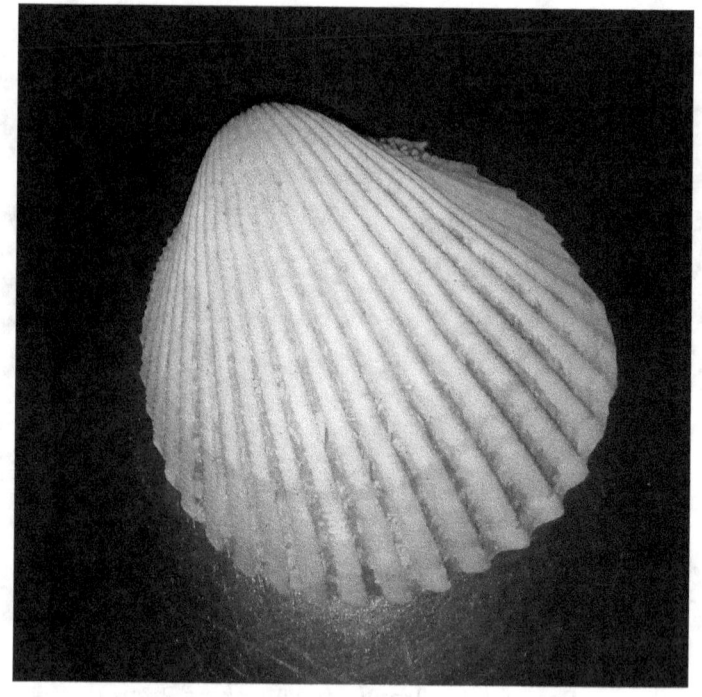

Shell Shocked? By this Stunning Shell.

SNAIL

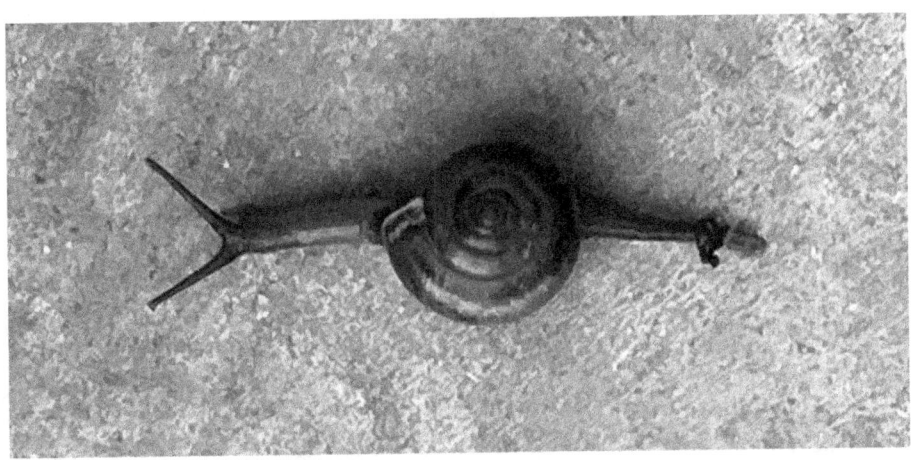

Snail. Head like Nail. And a Long Tail.

CARICATURE

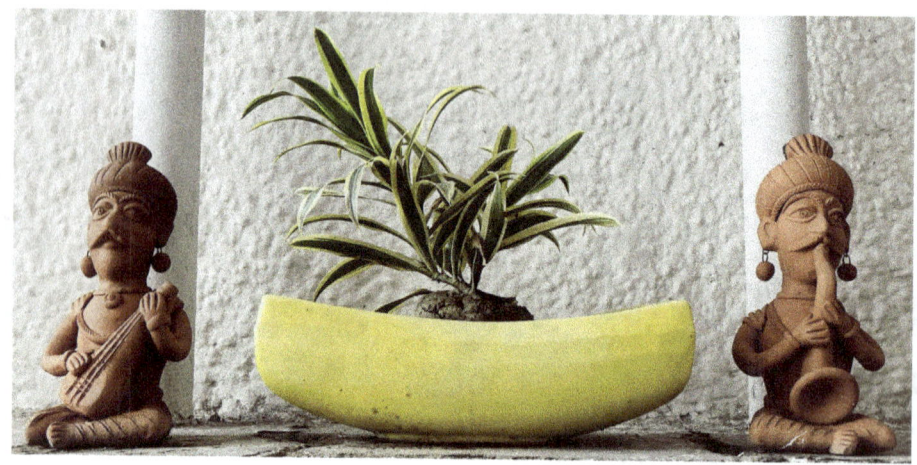

Caricature. Music in the Nature.

COLOR CANDOR

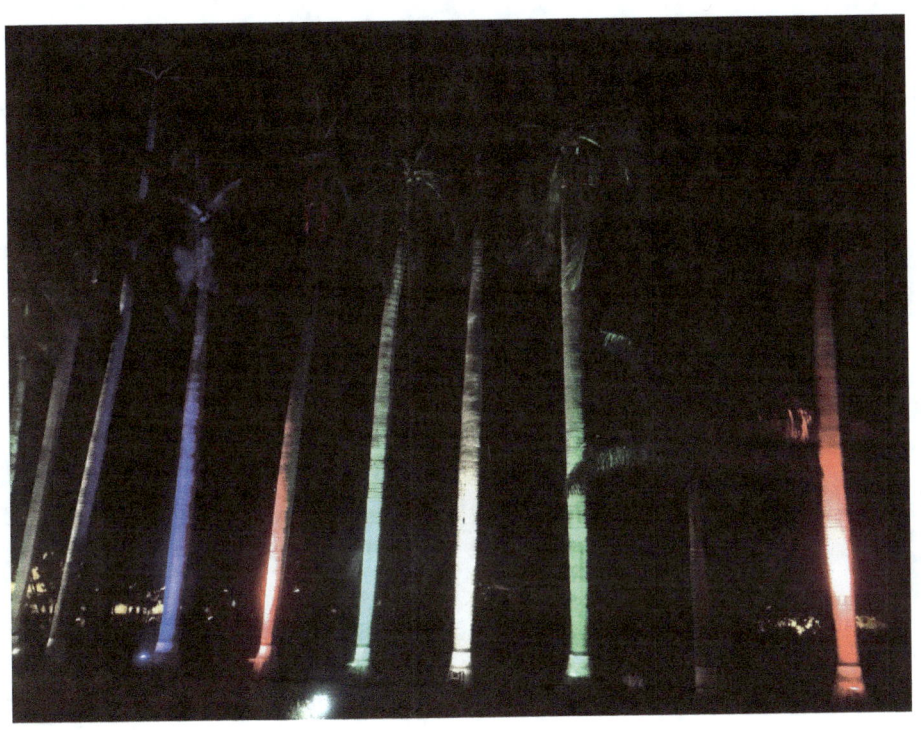

Many Shades of Light. Shining Sight.

CANINE CONFERENCE

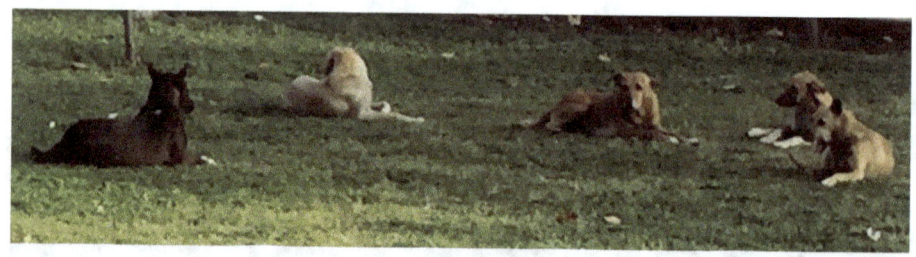

Canine Conference. No Consensus. Three versus Two.

WATERMARK

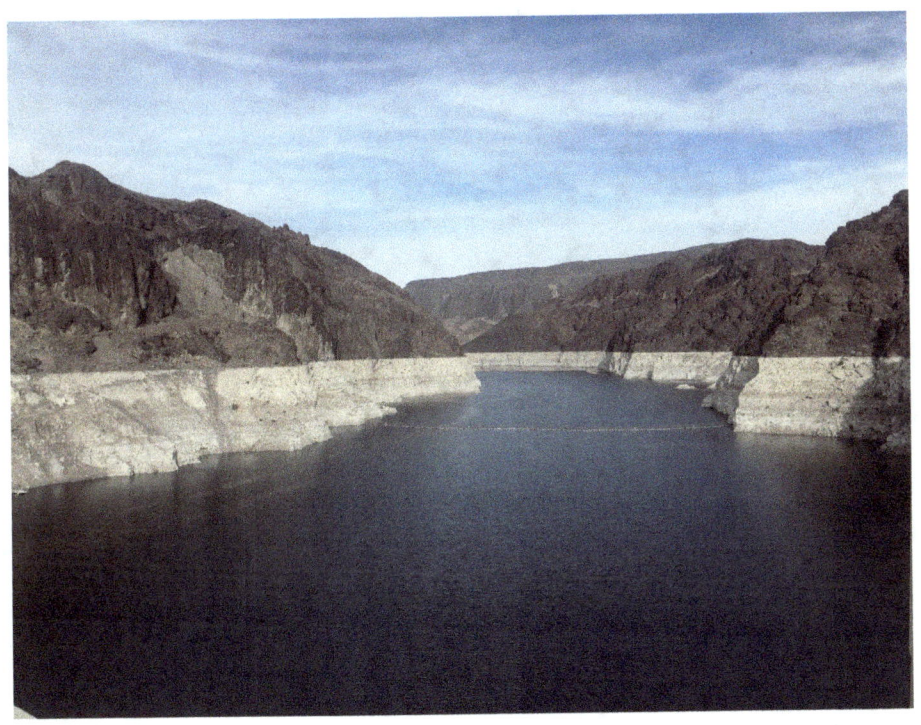

Watermark or Hallmark?

TURNING BACK

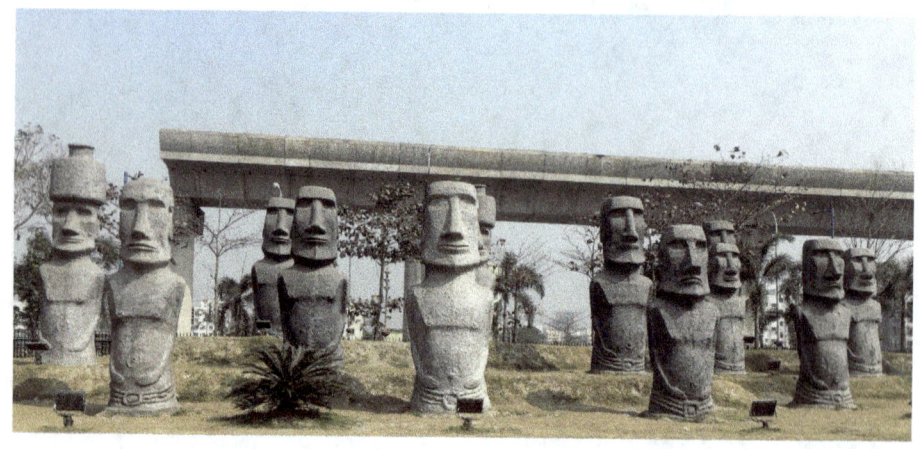

Bridging the Gap? Turning back. Please Don't Sack. We'll be back.

MOUNTAIN TOWN

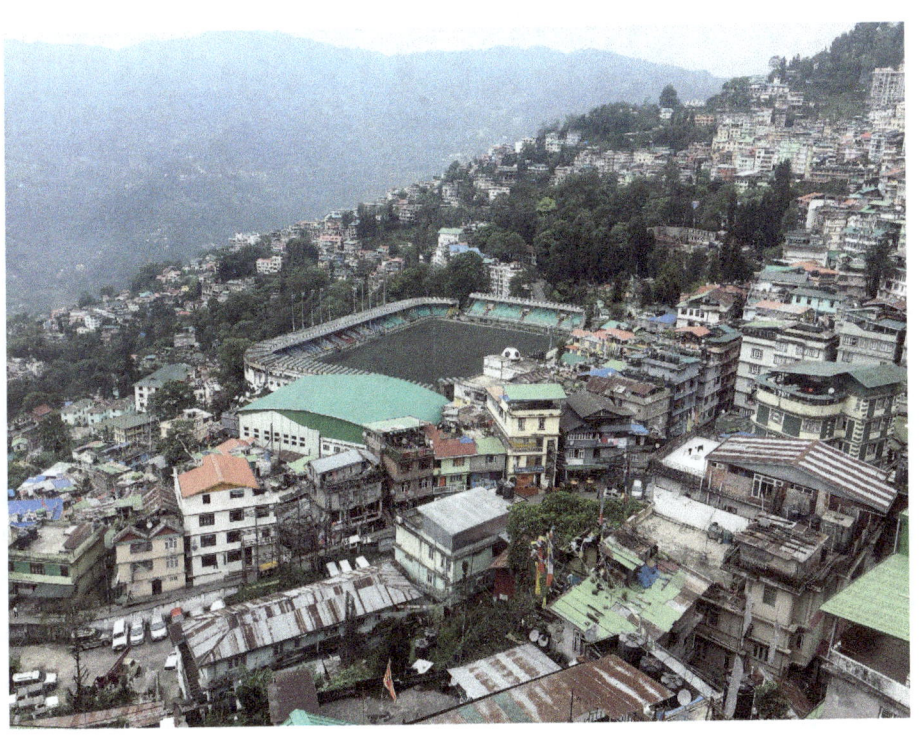

A beautiful landscape of a Mountain Town.

BEACH N PALM

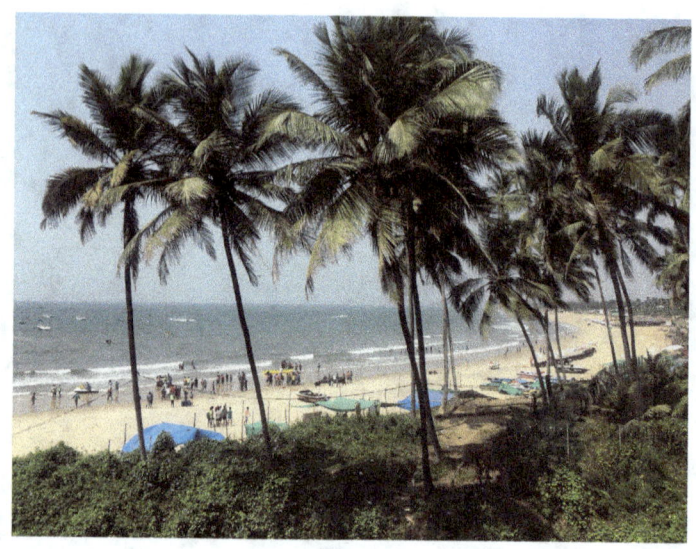

Beach and Palm. The Sea is Calm.

BLACK N WHITE

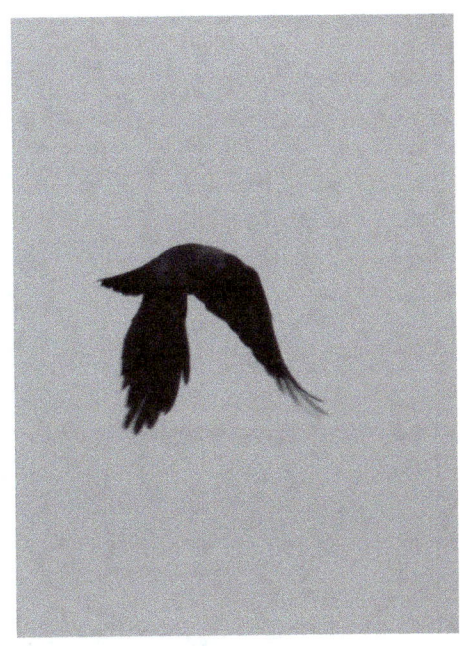

Black or White. Everything is Right.

CLOUD DRIFT

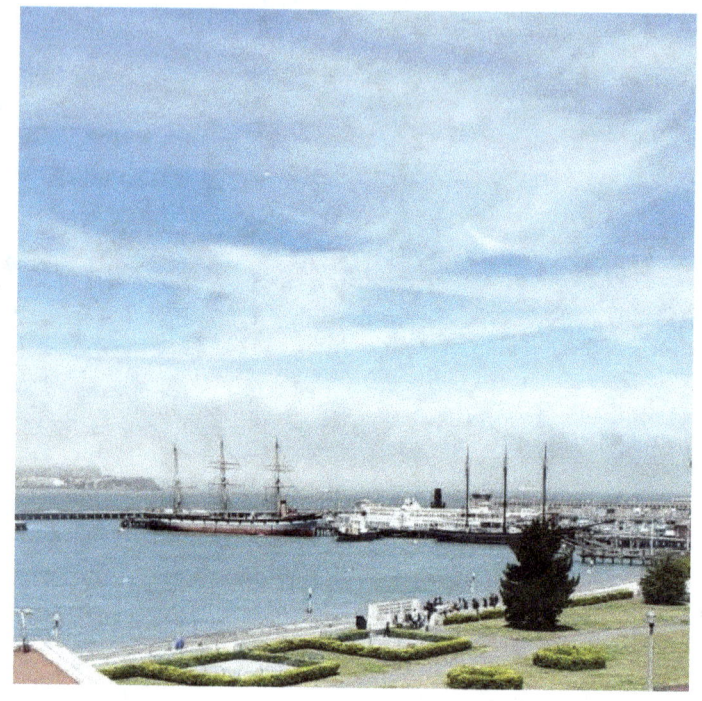

Ships sailing on the Sea and Clouds in the Sky

THE SUNSET AND SEA

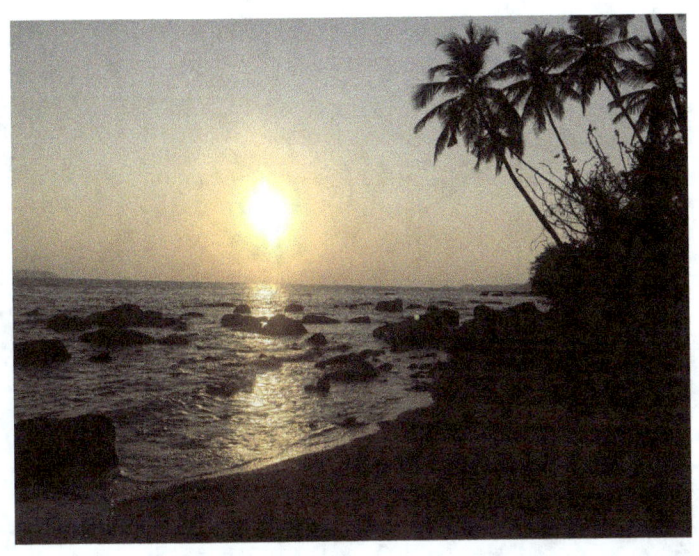

See the Sea. And the Sunset

HOME COMING

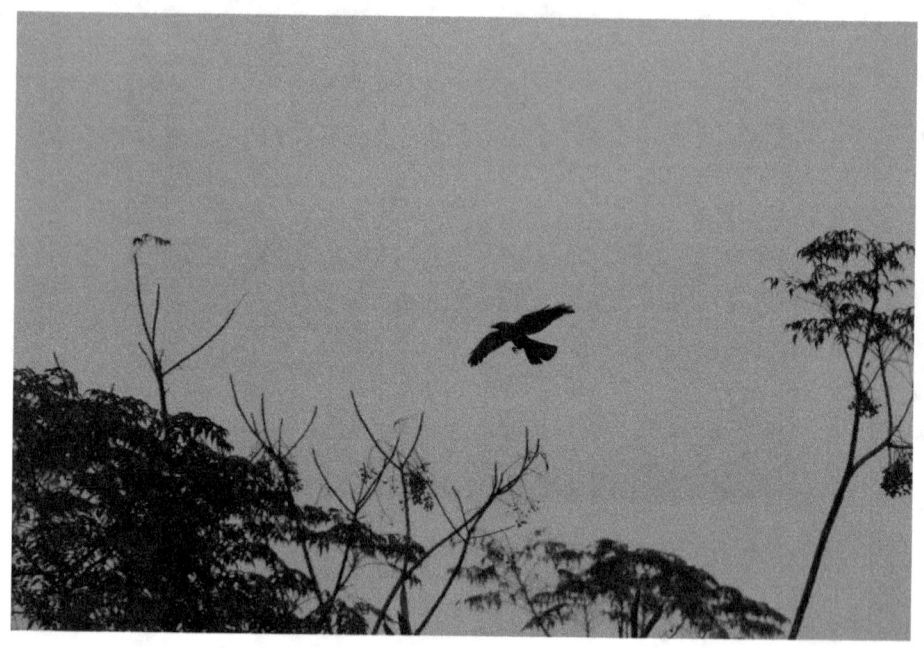

This bird is flying back home- before dark.

RAINBOW

The Silver Lining - in the Sky

FLOWER POWER

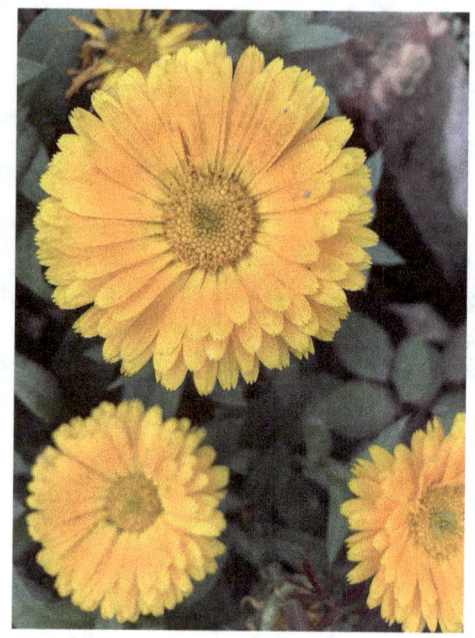

These Sun Flowers -are yelling Yellow

RUINS IN RED

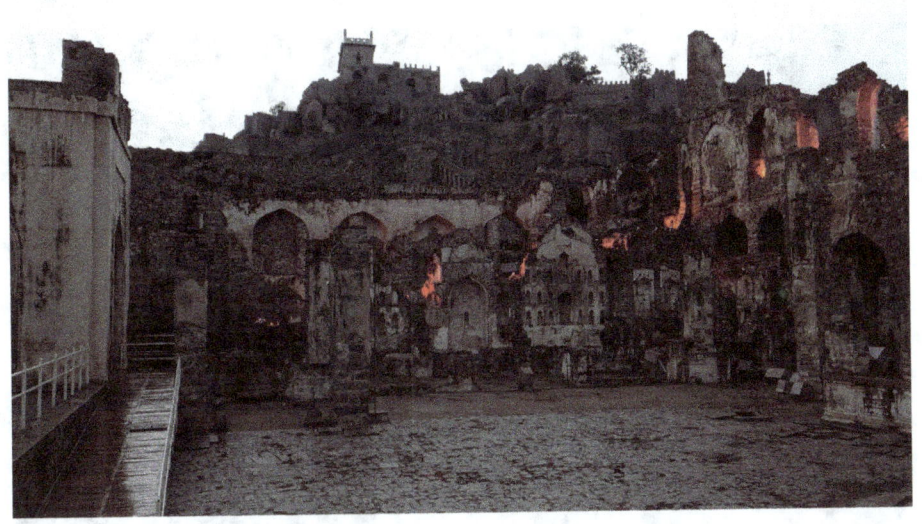

*This Damaged and Destructed Dwelling
is still Steadfast and Standing.*

DANCE AND DELIGHT

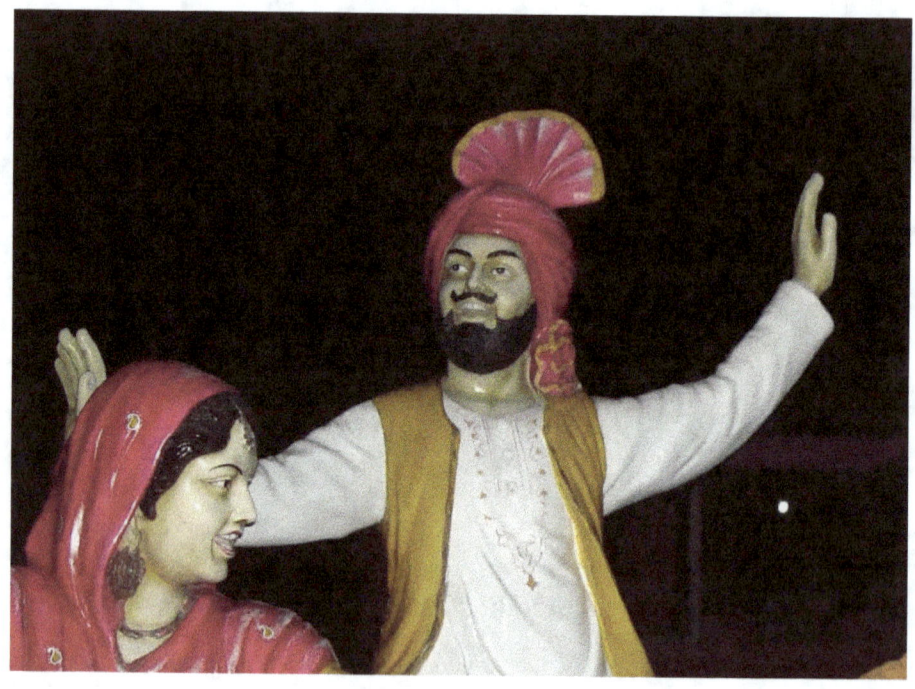

This couple is performing popular folk Punjabi Dance called Bhangra - in Delight.

THE SUN DIVING INTO DARKNESS

The Sun Diving into Darkness. Leaving behind Golden Trail - telling us the Divine Message - Let's Rest.

THE GUARD

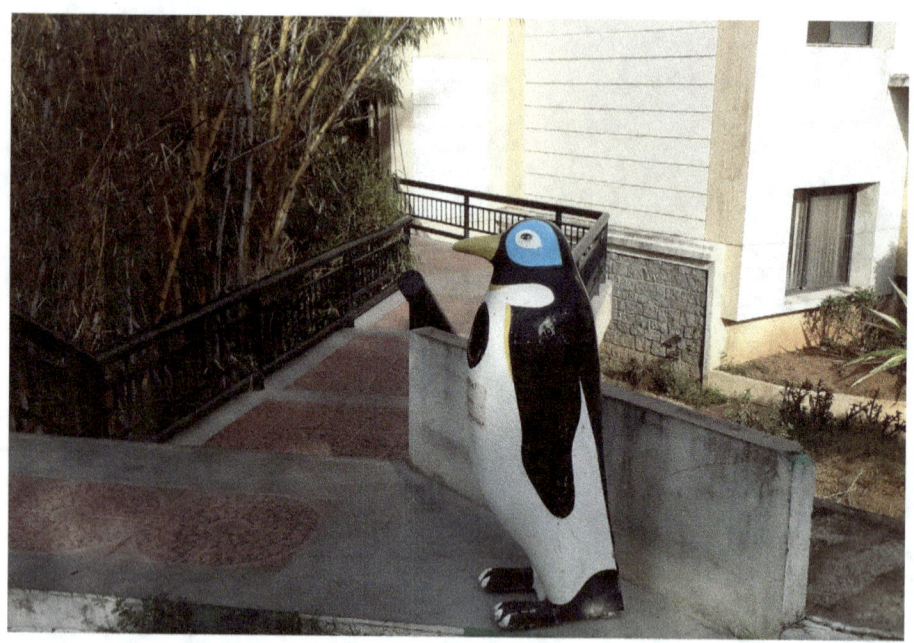

The Guard at the Gate.

SHRUBS AND SUNSET

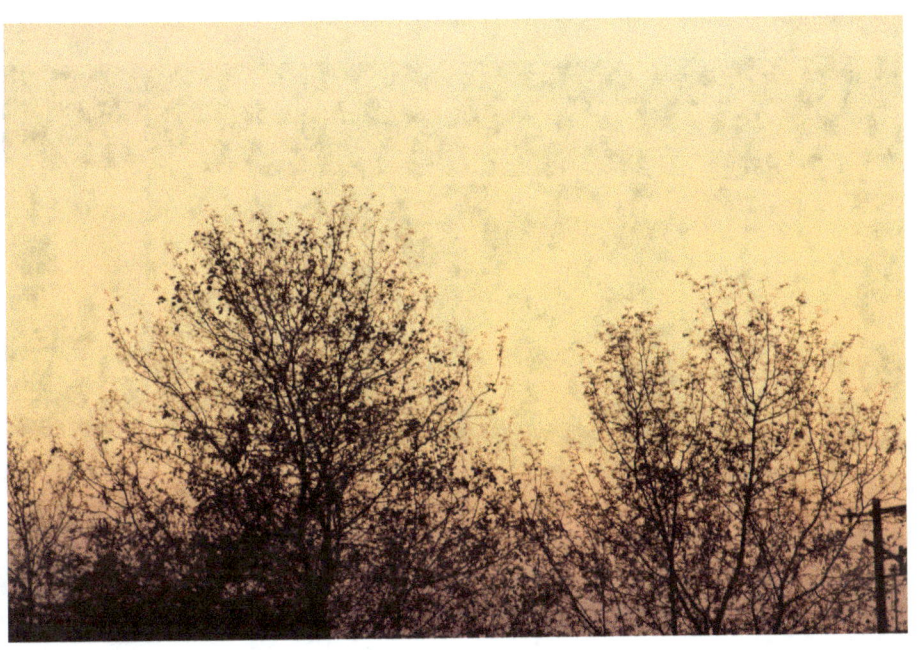

A Spectacular view of Shrubs in the backdrop of Golden Color of the Sunset.

GOLDEN AGE

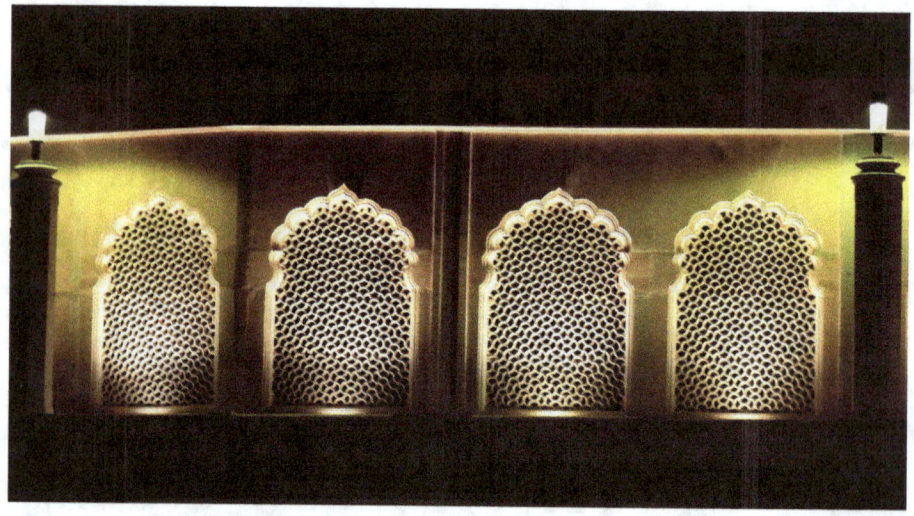

This wonderful Window reminds us of Golden Days.

FLYING COLORS

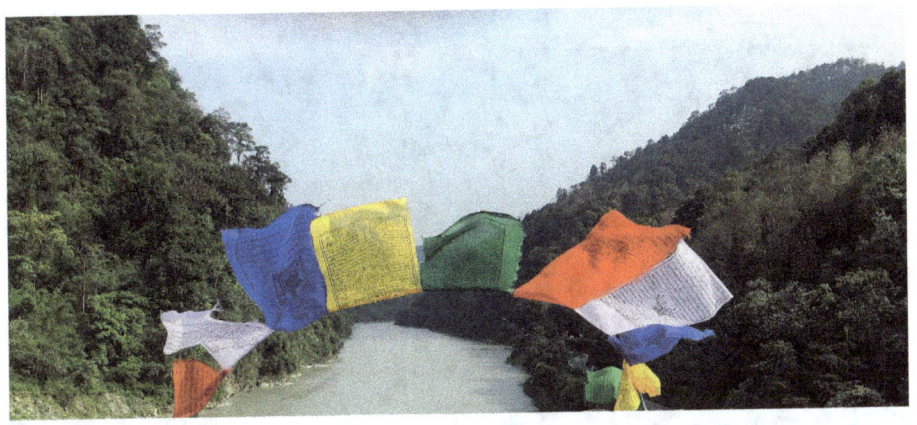

Nature has created this wonderful creation with flying colors.

MUSTARD FLOWER

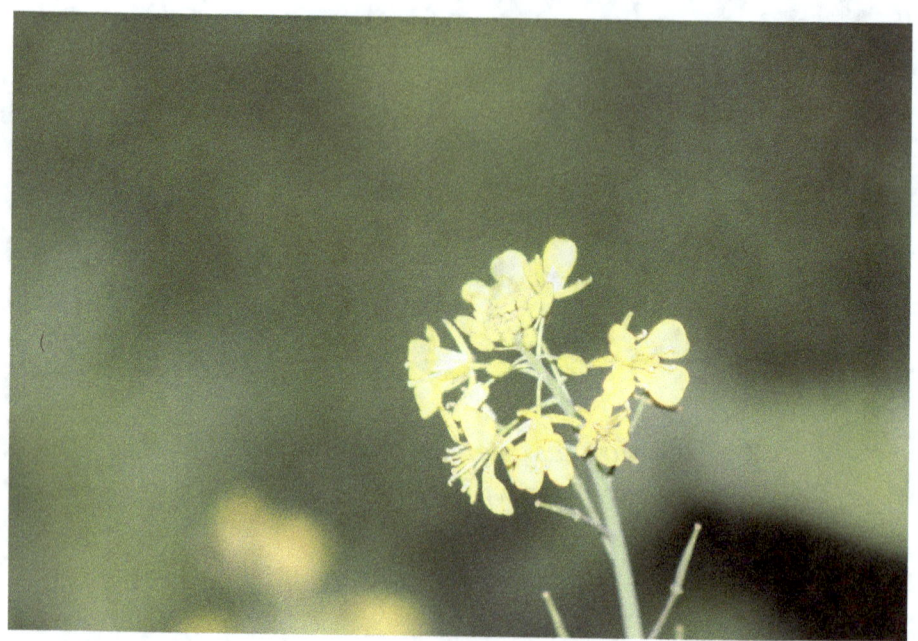

Must See this Magnificent Mustard Flower.

PUPPET AT PLAY

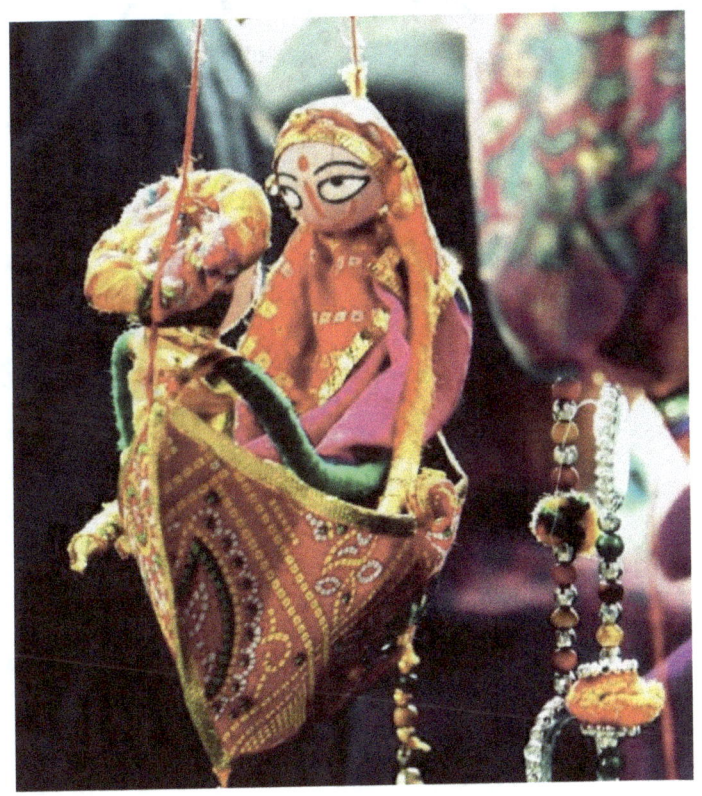

Puppet at Play. Likes to Sway.

TIME-PIECE OF ADVICE

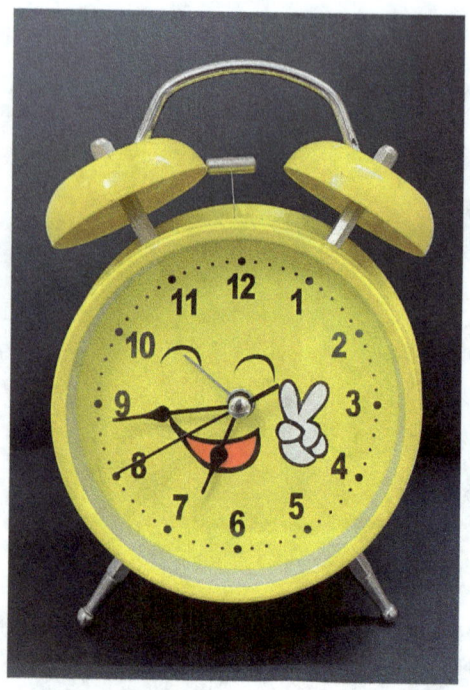

Dost thou love life? Then do not squander time for that's the stuff life is made of – Benjamin Franklin

SCENIC SEASHORE

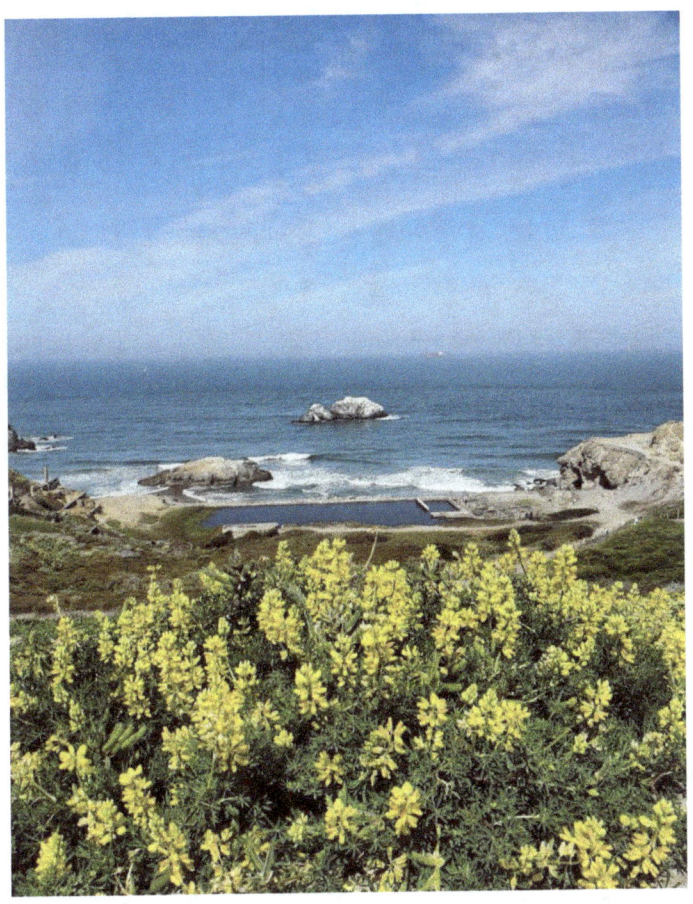

Scenic Seashore. Can you locate the Stone resembling the Alligator?

BE YOUR BEST CREATIVE SELF

ABOUT THE AUTHOR

J S Chahal

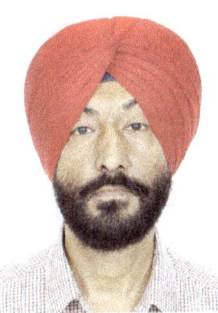

An Engineer - Solving drinking water scarcity - providing sanitation solutions to the rural residents. An ardent Peace lover. Focused on human flourishing. Creative thinker. Loves Reading. And Writing - that inspires individuals.

For more reading, please visit:
https://flourish.tips

BOOKS BY THIS AUTHOR

Inspirit

INSPIRIT is a rare collection of remarkable quotes blended with strikingly lifelike pictures. Powerful and inspiring words have profound impact on mind. When combined with pictures, its effect on brain is magnified and multiplied.

This collection of rare and inspiring quotes will uplift you, inspire you and boost your morale to achieve your personal and professional goals and objectives.

Powerful words and images will leave an imperishable impression on your mind. Its long-lasting motivational effect – will enable you, to live a life to its full potential.

The positive impact of these quotes will unleash your creativity – renew, replenish, revitalize you – and reduce stress.

You will be bewitched by bold words and beautiful pictures.

Each Quote will excite, encourage, energize, and enthuse you – each day.

This War Must Stop

February 24, 2022 – Russia-Ukraine war started. Since then, news channels all over the world, are showing horrifying pictures of horror and harm unleashed by the brutal blast of bombs. Missiles mauling mankind. Hypersonics hitting humankind. Rockets ravaging skyscrapers into rubble and ruins. Bombs burning the buildings. Tanks targeting theatres. Troops tearing down towns. Death and destruction everywhere....

Propelling This Planet To Prosperity Through Peace

If war is not a human part of nature, then why do we fight with others? Other communities? And other countries?

Make Your Voice Heard With Words

Words and Language have a profound effect on the minds of the audience. Choice of effective, right, and proper words while communicating can bring about transformational changes, produce desired results and improve business processes.

Children Daily Planner

Children Daily Planner

The Women Warriors

In this sleepy hamlet of district Ludhiana, Punjab – named village Hawas, inhabited mostly by middle to low-income residents, when officials of the department of water supply and sanitation (DWSS) talked to the gathering comprising men, women, and children about open defecation and its ill-effects, most of them started laughing, some women covered their faces with 'dupattas' feeling shy. Children were smiling facing each other.

Rating Hmb Tornado Using Ef Scale

On March 02, 2015 a tornado hit the near village Hambran

of district Ludhiana, Punjab. The roaring, swirling winds accompanied by lighting tilted Electric Transmission Line Poles, uprooted trees and blow away the roof panels and damaged houses. Wind speeds associated with the tornado could not be measured directly due to absence of any recording facility available in the area, hence, EF-Scale has been used to rate the tornado on EF-Scale and estimate its wind speed.

An Implementation Success Story Swachh Bharat Mission

Nearly, 60 crore Indians are defecating in open and excrete 65,000 tonnes of faeces into the environment each day, thereby making India number one open defecation country in the world.

Research Papers On Wind Engineering

Severe winds cause tremendous damage on structures. With the emergence of new generation tall structures which are remarkably flexible and low in damping the problem becomes more significant. Consequently, the effects of wind on structures are required to be considered more precisely than was previously required. Keeping above objective in mind the present study was undertaken to study the wind behavior.

Research Papers On Wind Engineering (Paperback)

Severe winds cause tremendous damage to structures. With the emergence of a new generation of tall structures which are remarkably flexible and low in damping the problem becomes more significant. Consequently, the effects of wind on structures are required to be considered more precisely than was previously required. Keeping the above objective in mind the present study was undertaken to study the wind behavior.

LOOKING FORWARD TO YOUR VISIT AT

www.ingramcontent.com/pod-product-compliance
Lightning Source LLC
Chambersburg PA
CBHW070259220526
45465CB00004B/1671